Leila Samadi Rendy
Iranian Diaspora Literature of Women

Studien zum Modernen Orient

herausgegeben
von Gerd Winkelhane

Studien zum Modernen Orient 28

Leila Samadi Rendy

Iranian Diaspora Literature of Women

KLAUS SCHWARZ VERLAG · BERLIN

Bibliographic Information of Deutsche Nationalbibliothek
Deutsche Nationalbibliothek registers this publication in the
Deutsche Nationalbibliografie; detailed bibliographical data
can be accessed at *http://dnb.ddb.de*.

Cover pic by L. Samadi Rendy

www.klaus-schwarz-verlag.com

© 2017 by Klaus Schwarz Verlag GmbH Berlin
First edition
Producer: J2P Berlin
Printed in Germany on chlorine-free bleached paper
ISBN 978-3-87997-457-3

For My Father

Abstract

Some years before and after the Islamic revolution in Iran in 1979, a huge number of Iranians migrated to western countries due to social and political problems. There is a significant body of literary and auto-biographical works by Iranian writers in the Diaspora during the last 50 years. The early works are mostly social and political, as writing about the private lives has been taboo, even in the diaspora. These literary writings has been analysed in Western academia to get a closer view of the political and social conditions in Iran before and after the Islamic revolution. However, in the last two decades, more literary and autobiographical works have been concerned with the private aspect of the lives of the characters in the Diaspora and the (trans)formation of their identity and the linguistic and cultural hybridity. This hybridity and the identity issues become more significant in the works of wo-men writers, as they are doubly marginalised as immigrants in the host land and second sex within patriarchy. There have been only a few critical works on the recent literary and autobiographical works of Iranian female writers in the Diaspora. This work examines the relationship between space, bilingualism, and writing, and female characters' identity formation in the late literary productions of Iranian women in the Diaspora, using post-colonial and postmodern theories of bilingualism, space, autobiography and gender.

In this research, the works of poetry and prose published in the anthology *Let Me Tell You Where I've Been: New Writing by Women of the Iranian Diaspora*, edited by Persis M. Karim (2006), and the full text of four memoirs, extracts from which are included in this work, are chosen for the case study.

The first theme of this research is the significance of space and displacement in the selected literary works. Here the private space of home and the public spaces of city and homeland, and their significance for the gendered identity of the female characters, has been examined using post-colonial and post-modern theories.

The second focus of this research is bilingualism and its role in the formation of the gendered identity of the female characters and narrators of the selected literary works. The generation and the community to which the subjects are connected shape their identity and investments in language and cultural capital. This leads to the creation of a personal English among the female characters and the use of English to refer to specific subjects requiring the freedom associated with this language.

The last theme of this research is the role of writing in identity formation of the female characters and the characteristics of the selected autobiographies and literary works of Iranian women in the diaspora. As the narrators in some texts claim, they write to recover from traumas and as a defense method against shame feelings. Besides, the subject searches for her 'self' in the process of writing. Stories of mothers and motherhood as complements of the narratives of self, and expression of personal theories to avoid inferiorization are of other themes of these works.

TABLE OF CONTENTS

Acknowledgements

The present book has been prepared as a thesis submitted for the degree of Doctor of Philosophy from the Institute of Iranian Studies, Georg-August University of Göttingen. Special thanks are due to my advisor Prof. Dr. Philip Kreyenbroek, director of this institute for the continuous support of my Ph.D study and related research, for his patience, motivation, and immense knowledge. His expertise has been extremely valuable, and without him this project would not have been possible. Also I would like to express my sincere gratitude to my second advisor PD Dr. Roxane Haag-Higuchi, University of Bamberg, for her insightful comments and encouragement. Also I would like to thank Prof. Dr. Gordon Whittaker, Institute of Ethnology, University of Göttingen, whose questions inspired me to widen my research from various perspectives.

Over the past four and a half years I have been extremely fortunate to receive both academic and financial support from a number of different institutions: I am indebted to Katholischer Akademischer Ausländer-Dienst (KAAD) for the financial support they gave me for three years. I have also benefited greatly from the courses and grants of Graduiertenschule für Geisteswissenschaften Göttingen (GSGG) since the very first days of my work. The publication of the present book is also financed by GSGG.

Thanks are also extended to Prof. Dr. Brigitte Glaser, Institute of English Studies, University of Göttingen, for allowing me the opportunity to discuss my methodology in the early stages of this work.

Finally, my special thanks go to my friends in Göttingen and my family; my father whose life was too short to let him see the results of all the sacrifices he made for me, my mother, my brothers and my dear husband, all of whom have given me encouragement, love and support throughout.

CHAPTER ONE: INTRODUCTION

Introduction and Case Study

In the last 50 years, a large population of Iranians has left for western countries in search of better social and political conditions. The most studied literary works of the Iranian Diaspora are the social and political ones by authors who migrated as adults a few years before or after the Islamic revolution. However, these works, and the studies carried out on them, have not provided us with adequate information on and analysis of the relationship between the language and the gendered identity of the characters and narrators. The recent literary works and memoirs of Iranian writers in the Diaspora reflect the (trans)formation of gendered identity and the linguistic and cultural hybridity of the diasporic characters. This hybridity and the identity issues become more significant in the case of women, as they are doubly "colonialised", in Spivak's term, due to discrimination as colonial subjects in the Diaspora and gender subordination within patriarchy (Spivak 1994: 103).

The literary works and memoirs of Iranian women in the Diaspora are written in both Farsi and the language of the host land. As there is a huge population of Iranians living in the English speaking countries, a great number of these works are in English, embodying identity and gender issues. Studying these works can help the academic world get a better understanding of the relationship between language acquisition, gender and generation, and also the aspects of the transformation of English among Iranian female characters in the Diaspora.

In this book I will analyze all the literary genres produced in English by the second generation Iranian women in the diaspora. Therefore, I have chosen an anthology of poetry and prose by Iranian diasporic female authors entitled *Let Me Tell You Where I've Been: New Writing by Women of the Iranian Diaspora*, edited by Persis M. Karim

(2006) as the main part of the case study of this research. The other existing anthologies, for example *A World Between: Poems, Short Stories, and Essays by Iranian-Americans* (Karim 1999) or *Tremors: New Fiction by Iranian American Writers* (Amirrezvani, Karim 2013) either include the works of male authors and do not focus on the main themes of female writers, or are limited to one genre.

The case study of this research also includes the full text of four memoirs, excerpts of which are published in the anthology *Let Me Tell You Where I've Been: New Writing by Women of the Iranian Diaspora* (Karim 2006). The memoirs are entitled *Lipstick Jihad: A Memoir of Growing Up Iranian in America and American in Iran* (Moaveni 2006), *Saffron Sky: A Life Between Iran and America* (Asayesh 2002), *To See and See Again: A Life in Iran and America* (Bahrampour 1999), and *Funny in Farsi: A Memoir of Growing Up Iranian in America* (Dumas 2004). As autobiography is one of the main genres of the literature of Iranian diasporic female writers, I decided to study the full texts to be able to analyse the different themes they incorporate. Of course, there are several memoirs and autobiographies in English by the second generation of Iranian female authors in the diaspora as listed in Appendix I. However, I limited the study to the four above mentioned works as they embody the main themes of the literature of second generation diasporic Iranian authors. Works which focus on a ethnic or religious minority, for example Saba Soomekh's *From the Shahs to Los Angeles: Three generations of Iranian Jewish women between religion and culture* (2013), are not discussed here as I have tried to work on the more general idea of Iranian cultural identity and Iranianness.

Funny in Farsi by Firoozeh Dumas is the story of Firoozeh, a seven year old girl who moved from Iran to Whittier, California, with her parents, Kazem and Nazireh, and her brothers. Her father studied in America at a graduate school in Texas. He believed that America is the country for him and his family. Therefore, trusting his knowledge of English and American culture, he takes his family with him to America in search of a better life. However, his language skills are very limited and Firoozeh has to adjust to American culture by herself, and even help her family in this way, leading to many humorous and awkward situations.

The memoir follows Firoozeh and her family as she goes through difficult situations such as trying to learn the language and earn money, marrying a Frenchman, and the anti-Iranian atmosphere in America during and after the Iranian Hostage Crisis. Dumas uses an ironic tone even in the most painful moments.

In *Saffron Sky* by Gelareh Asayesh a young journalist, "Gelareh", tells the story of her immigration from Iran in 1977, her integration in the American culture as a teenager, and her return to her homeland in October 1990 during the Iran-Iraq war. Asayesh combines the reporter's objective point of view with poetic and subjective descriptions and emotional analysis. She describes the clash between the Iranian people's support for its traditional, "religious" government and its interest in a modern, globalized life style, and the way it affects the women's daily life. However, the main setting of this memoir is America. Gelareh refers to the struggles of growing up in Chapel Hill, her search for her gendered identity between two worlds, and her attempt to make a connection between her homeland and her new identity as an American.

"Tara", the main character of *To See and See Again* by Tara Bahrampour, and her family arrived in America when she was eleven years old. Her American mother and Iranian father fled from the Islamic Revolution in Iran. In the 1990s, she goes back to Iran as an adult to visit her extended family and experience the world she might have grown up in. One of the main themes of this memoir is the condition of three generations of a privileged Iranian family before, during and after the revolution. Besides, the memoir focuses on the life of the characters in the diaspora. The author describes the Iran of her childhood, her family's attempt to lead a working-class life in Oregon and her return to post-revolution Iran, where she experiences the secret "underground" life many people are engaged in, and visits her family's lost empire, as she tries to discover how to synthesize both worlds. Analytically and poetically, *To See and See Again* manifests the complications of the modern immigrant experience as well as providing an image of Iran in the time of transformation.

Lipstick Jihad by Azadeh Moaveni starts with the story of Azadeh's childhood in America, longing for the homeland. As an adult and the reporter for *Time* magazine she lived in Tehran for two years. There she witnessed clashes between the people and the Islamic government which sought to impose rigid Islamic rules on modern life. However, the younger generation in Iran had learned to get around these rules and was leading an underground Western life. Many women rebelled against the restrictions in clothing and behavior by wearing makeup and covering their hair only partially. All journalists were working under the control of Iranian intelligence agents, and their articles had to be approved or partially censored before publication. Azadeh had to leave the country, as she could not tolerate the suppression and fear anymore. However, she understands that she belongs in both Iran and America.

The aim of this research is to analyse the main themes of the selected literary and autobiographical works of Iranian women in the Diaspora, which include gendered identity and the condition of female characters, using post-modern and post-colonial theories of space, bilingualism, autobiography and gender. I have only been able to compare the identity issues and struggles of male and female characters where the narrators of the selected works have referred to this subject. In this work the effects of the spaces of home, city and homeland on the gendered identity of the female characters of the selected literary works will be explored. Besides, the relationship between second language acquisition and the gendered roles of the female diasporic characters of different generation will be studied. Moreover, the creation of personal English and the use of English to refer to taboos and secrets among female characters will be discussed. Finally, the role of writing in the identity formation of the implied authors of the works and other female characters will be analyzed. The works of fiction and poetry which are included in the case study have mostly autobiographical elements and will be studied using the postcolonial theories of autobiography and gender, as by the memoirs in the case study. This research can be a step toward a better understanding of the form and content of some of the latest literary and autobiographical productions of Iranian female writers in the Diaspora.

Research Questions

As mentioned above, in this research post-colonial and post-modern theories of space, bilingualism and autobiography will be applied to the recent literary productions of Iranian female writers in the Diaspora, which focus on identity and gender from different perspectives and have been rarely studied theoretically. The aim of this research is to find answers to the following questions:

Are the narrators of these works speaking with cultural accent? Do the characters feel lost between two worlds? Have they found a new home, having been integrated into western culture? What are the roles of the three spaces of home, city and homeland in the formation and transformation of the gendered identity of the female characters? Does the flow of global space into the local ones affect the gendered identity of female characters living in Iranian cities?

How does the experience of migration manifest itself in language? What is the difference between second language learning for the two generations of female characters in the diaspora? How are the experiences of the first and second generation characters different in terms of second language acquisition? What are the characteristics of the English the characters use among themselves or to narrate their life stories? What is the significance of the use of the English among the second generation characters? Is the translation of self through language possible?

What is the significance of the act of narrating for the implied authors and characters of the selected works? What are the concerns of Iranian female writers in the Diaspora and their understanding of the lives of female subjects both in Iran and in the western world? What are the characteristics of these works and in what sense are they different from the first autobiographical works of Iranian Women in the Diaspora?

Background of the Study and Review of Literature

Although post-colonial theories are widely used to analyze Diaspora literary works, few researches have been carried out on the late literary works and memoirs of Iranian female writers in the Diaspora. This book aims to fill this lacuna and give the literature of Iranian women in the Diaspora a voice in the academy.

The concept of gender is of great significance in diaspora studies. An important reason for this, among other factors, may be the key role of women in preserving and transferring the collective cultural identity of the diasporic community and/or their double-marginality in the diaspora as the second sex and immigrants. A considerable amount of research has been done on the gendered identity and roles of female subjects of different diasporas, with or without colonial background. Some of the important works on the question of gender in Asian diasporas are *Negotiating Identities: Women in the Indian Diaspora* by Aparna Rayaprol (1997), *Cross-Border Marriages: Gender and Mobility in Transnational Asia* by N. Constable (2005) and *Spaces of Their Own: Women's Public Sphere in Transnational China* edited by M. Yang (1999). On the women of European and South American diasporas are works such as *Women and the Irish Diaspora* by B. Gray (2004), *Transnational America: Feminisms, Diasporas, Neoliberalisms* by I. Grewal (2005) and *Transnational Tortillas: Race, Gender, and Shop-Floor Politics in Mexico and the United States* by C. Bank Muñoz (2008) published. Besides nationality, race and religion are main common grounds in the formation of collective identity in diasporic communities. The Muslim,

Jewish or Black diasporas, and the role and condition of women in them, have achieved the attentions of many scholars. *Geographies of Muslim Identities: Diaspora, Gender and Belonging* edited by C. Aitchison, P. Hopkins, and M.-P. Kwan (2007), *Jewish Portraits, Indian Frames: Women's Narratives from a Diaspora of Hope* by Jael Miriam Silliman (2001) and *Women and Religion in the African Diaspora: Knowledge, Power, and Performance* edited by R. M Griffith, and B. D. Savage (2006) are among the most influential studies carried out in this field.

The concept of space, which includes a network of relations occurring in a specific place and time (Massey 1992: 80–81), has recently received a great deal of attention in social and literary studies in Western academia. Sexual identity and body politics can be transformed by the space the subjects are connected to (Grosz 1997: 239). Julia Kristeva in "Women's Time" (1986) and bell hooks in *Feminist Theory from Margin to Center* (1984) have referred to the significance of the association of female subjects with the space of home in the formation of their gendered identity and the expectations of the community. Pamela Gilbert in "Sex and the Modern City" (2009) and Fran Tonkiss in *Space, the City and Social Theory* (2005) have theorized the effects of urban freedom on the transformation of sexual identity of female subjects. Also Benedict Anderson in *Imagined Communities* (1991) has mentioned the importance of the influence of globalism on the gendered identity of the subjects. Salman Rushdie in *Imaginary Homelands* (1991) on a literary level, and Homi Bhabha in *The Location of Culture* (1994) on a theoretical level have written on the subject of homeland, cultural identity and gender, and the way the space of homeland goes through changes in the post-modern era.

Although a certain amount of theoretical work has been done on space and gendered identity in the Diaspora and the globalized world, little has been done on the sexuality of Iranian women in the Diaspora. *Diasporic Narratives of Sexuality: Identity Formation among Iranian-Swedish Women,* by Fataneh Farahani (2007) and *Muslim Diaspora in the West: Negotiating Gender, Home and Belonging* edited by Haideh

Moghissi, Halleh Ghorashi (2010) focus on the way sexual identity of Iranian females has changed in western societies. Their findings are based on interviews, and therefore may not offer evidence regarding taboo subjects.

On the changes in sexual politics of Iranian women in the homeland in the last few decades, a few works have been published, including *Women and Politics in Iran: Veiling, Unveiling and Reveiling* by Hamideh Sedghi (2007) and *Sexual Politics in Modern Iran* By Janet Afary (2009), and *Passionate Uprisings: Iran's Sexual Revolution* by Pardis Mahdavi (2009). However, in the present writer's view these case studies are too subjective in their theoretical approach to the reasons and results of the transformation of sexual identity in contemporary Iran.

Bilingualism and gendered identity in the communities in the Diaspora has been studied theoretically by Bonny Norton and A. Pavlenko in *Gender and English Language Learners* (2004). Norton, in her essays with Carolyn McKinney (2011), has analyzed the cultural investment of the subjects in the diasporic community or natives of the hostland, and the consequences of their choice. However, there have only been few theoretical studies on the representation of the linguistic experiences of female characters in the literary works of Iranian female writers in the Diaspora. Babak Elahi in "Translating the Self" focuses on the importance of Farsi for the members of Iranian Diaspora and analyses a few memoirs of Iranians in the Diaspora. He writes:

> In Iranian national culture, Persian is both a common tongue and the repository for a long-honored tradition of poetry, including the generally pre-Islamic themes of Iran's great national epic, Ferdowsi's Shahnameh. Today, Persian—as an ethnolinguistic essence, as a cultural performance, and as an epistemological framework—continues to be important for Iranian exiles in the United States and elsewhere (Elahi 2006: 464).

Besides, Daniel Grassian in *Iranian and Diasporic Literature in the 21st Century* (2013) gives a general view of the latest literary productions of

Iranians, both in Iran and in the Diaspora, referring to the subject of language and bilingualism briefly.

Very little work has been done on the way gendered identity in the Diaspora and homeland is reported by Iranian women in their memoirs. In *Veils and Words* (Milani 1992) there is an analysis of the first autobiographies of Iranian women in Iran and in the Diaspora which mostly focus on the social and political lives of the authors. Amy Motlagh in "Towards a Theory of Iranian American Life Writing" explains the differences between the memoirs of first and second generation female writers, and analyses a few works by the latter which are concerned with the private aspects of the lives of the characters. Also Sanaz Fotouhi in *Literature of the Iranian Diaspora: Meaning and Identity since the Islamic Revolution* studies the identity issues of the characters of some diasporic works, but the work is mostly descriptive and subjective. In *Constructing Identity in Iranian-American Self-Narrative* Maria D. Wagenknecht analyses the process of identity formation through writing, but refers to the specific identity problems of the female subjects briefly. Besides, poetry and short autobiographical prose have not been analyzed in this works. However, it can be considered the first theoretical work which contributes to the understanding of the common identity issues of the Iranian-American diasporic characters.

Methods and Outline

Exile is a situation in which one is forced by the authorities to leave one's country or home and go to live in a foreign country. The characters I have analyzed in my work have chosen to leave the country freely in search of a better social, political and financial situation, so the term exile would not apply here. However, there are a few theorists I referred to here, and also characters in the literary works under discussion, who use the term exile loosely for the condition of unforced leaving the homeland.

On the other hand, Diaspora "involves dwelling, maintaining communities, having collective homes away from home (and in this it is different from exile, with its frequently individualistic focus)" (Clifford 1994, 308). The characters I study here have a strong relationship with the community of Iranians abroad and their identities are (trans)formed in accordance with its norms and expectations. Therefore, they are not individual exiles but social diasporic subjects. Using the term Diaspora allows me to study the collective identity of all the generations (first generation characters which left Iran as adults and the second generation characters which are brought up and/or born in a foreign country) of the community of Iranian characters abroad.

Besides, as Ghorashi in *Ways to Survive, Battles to Win* declares "unlike exile, diasporic understanding of homeland signifies not a place to return to but rather a domain that serves as one of the available discourses within present negotiations" (Ghorashi 2002, 106). Although homeland and visiting the left home is one of the main themes of the selected works of this research, but a permanent return is not desired by the characters under discussion. This makes Diaspora a more appropriate term to refer to the situation of the characters I studied here.

In this research the relationship between space, gender and identity in the lives of female characters of the literary productions of Iranian Women in the Diaspora, the role of bilingualism in their identity formation, and the significance of autobiography writing for their identity, as well as the stylistic characteristics of these autobiographies will be analyzed through the application of post-colonial and post-modern theories.

As Sanaz Fotouhi in *The Literature of the Iranian Diaspora: Meaning and Identity Since the Islamic Revolution* states, "[l]ike post-colonial writers, diasporic Iranian writers draw on elements of the past to transform them, rewrite them, to reconstruct themselves, their past and future, against colonial/domineering forces" (Fotouhi 15). Although Iran has never been a colony, the main themes of Iranian diasporic literature and the literature of diasporas with colonial background are alike. This may be due to the similarity of the authors' experiences of marginality in past and present.

Fotouhi uses the definition of colonialism by Elleke Boehmer, according to which "colonialism was not different from other kinds of authority, religious or political, in claiming a monopoly on definitions in order to control a [...] reality." In her book Fotouhi views "the unifying and totalitarian pre- and post-revolutionary regimes of Iran, as quasi-colonial and oppressive forces that have rendered many Iranians marginal both in Iran and abroad, and examines the specific techniques that writers use to draw on the past and to reflect and project a desired future" (Fotouhi 15-16). I will also use this argument in the present research, as I believe the condition of the characters and authors of the literature of Iranian diaspora resembles the literature of the post-colonial diaspora. That is why I will analyse the diasporic literature of Iranian diaspora using post-colonial theories.

The hybrid identities and in-between lives which are represented in the literature of the Iranian diapsora, are also the main focuses of the post-modern theories. B. Zielke and J. Straub in "Culture, Psychotherapy/Diasporic Self" (2008) refer to this issue as follows:

> The members of multi-ethnic and multi-cultural communities are seen as seismographs of postmodern living conditions. As a kind of avant-garde it is the migrants who show what affects, in today's pluralistic late modern world, all members of society. Postmodern concepts, such as 'relational' or 'dialogical self' (Gergen 1991; Hermans et al. 1993) too produce theory figures more or less tailored to diasporic existences (Zielke & Straub 64).

The post-modern theories of space, language, writing and gender can contribute to the investigation of the post modern selves and conditions of the characters of the Iranian diasporic literature. Therefore, I will apply these theories here to the selected works.

The first focus of this research is the influence of the spaces of home, city, homeland and global spaces on the gendered identity of female characters, as reflected in the selected literary works. The present study defines space as Doreen Massey formulated it in "Politics and Space/Time":

> 'Space' is created out of the vast intricacies, the incredible complexities of the interlocking and the non-interlocking, and the networks of relations at every scale from the global to the local. What makes a particular view of these social relations specifically spatial is their simultaneity. It is a simultaneity, also, which has extension and configuration (Massey 1992: 80–81).

Association and engagement with the private space of the home play an important role in the identity formation of the female subjects in the literary works in question, and affect their lives in the Diaspora in different ways. Living in a western city with the freedom it provides is a challenging experience for the female characters of the literary works of Iranian Diaspora women who have lived with the limitations in Iranian traditional cities, where traditional sexual norms reign. This causes sexual, religious and cultural identity crises. Besides, in the case of female characters living in Iran, globalized space and sexual identity play an important role in challenging the traditional understanding of body space. Finally, the space of homeland affects the sexual concept of the female characters, as transmitters and protectors of the value system of their culture.

For the Iranian female characters of the selected literary works, the "private space" of home is the place where the self is secure and protected. These characters have always associated themselves with the space of home, due to their limited access to public life. They feel a detachment from their identity and lose their selfhood when they are away from home in the Diaspora. They don't have a sense of belonging and origin and feel insecure in the new world and culture. Julia

Kristeva (1986) and bell hooks (1984) have written powerfully on the association of women with cyclical, ahistorical time and on the association of women with home as a place of refuge, and of origin. This place is often associated with the mother (and later, for Kristeva, the wife), and is likewise seen as a refuge from history—this time positively as a place where identity is absolute and protected. These theories can be traced in the representations of the attachment of the female subjects of the selected works to the space of home, which is left behind in homeland. The female characters are seen by themselves and the members of the diasporic community of Iranians as symbols of the unchanging home, and consequently, of an unchanging identity. Therefore, integration in the culture of the host land is a taboo for female characters in the Diaspora. This challenge is more significant when it comes to the young generation which longs to belong in the new free world.

Due to the separation of Iranian women from men in private and social life, and the restriction of the female domains to the home and a few public spaces, female subjects feel closer to each other and have a sense of collective identity. This extends to their perceptions of sexuality; they sit half- naked in public baths, compare breasts, talk with each other about the details of their body and sexual relations, and touch each other. Here the ideas of Kristeva will be applied to analyze the association of female characters and the space of home. She writes: "Women doubtless reproduce among themselves the strange gamut of forgotten body relationships with their mothers" (Kristeva 1986: 180). However, the sisterly relationship of Iranian female characters is interpreted as a sign of homosexual tendencies in western society, as shown by the works selected here. Therefore, in some cases the way the characters deal with the space of body goes through change in the Diaspora.

Another significant theme in the case study is the opposition between the modern urban spaces of western countries and the more traditional atmosphere of cities in Iran. The gendered identity of an Iranian female character in a traditional Iranian city differs from that of female characters in a western modern city. This affects the religious and sexual identity of the subjects and creates religious and ethic hybridity in the Diaspora. To explain this situation, the ideas of Pamela Gilbert in "Sex and the Modern City" (2009) will be used. She declares that modern western cities, due to the density and anonymity, make urban freedom uniquely possible. However, for the female characters living with this freedom, dangers are involved, such as victimization or prostitution, whereas the pleasures of the city, sexual or otherwise, are proffered through consumerist imagery (Gilbert 2009).

Freedom of mobility in urban space, which is more accessible for diasporic female characters in western cities, changes their sexual politics and understanding of body space. On the other hand, their sexual politics are considered main factors in their traditional national identity, and preserving it is very important for the community. Here the ideas of Elizabeth Wilson will be used to analyze the sexual identity of the characters and the expectations of the community in the Diaspora. She writes "women have fared especially badly in western visions of the metropolis because they have seemed to represent disorder. There is fear of the city as a realm of uncontrolled and chaotic sexual license, and the rigid control of women in cities has been felt necessary to avert this danger" (Wilson 1991: 157). Although religion and tradition have patriarchal tendencies and tend to repress female sexuality, some Iranian female characters decide to observe the Iranian Muslim tradition of chastity as a defense method. This is also a way of guaranteeing their belonging to the community of Iranians which plays an important role in the preservation of the identity of the character. However, among female characters born or brought up in the Diaspora, one often sees a detachment from Islamic values arising from the desire to enjoy the freedom of a western life and belong to the new world.

Lack of communication is reflected in the selected literary works as one of the main problems of female characters in the western cities.

Social interaction and communication in urban life is one of the great needs of the female subjects of these works, as they have got used to it in Iranian cities. Communication and human relations in western cities are generally far less intensive than in Iranian ones.

One of the most significant issues in the works in question is the sexual identity of female characters in Iran. The sexual politics of their own or other relatives are reported and commented on to give a clear picture of the centrality of sexuality for female characters in the religious and traditional urban space in Iran. Iranian cities as reported in these works are spaces in which religious and moral values reign and people are connected to each other. Observing traditional values and Islamic dress code and sexuality provides the subjects with a sense of safety.

It is not only in the Diaspora that space affects the sexual identity of female subjects. In the present global world, women's sexual understanding is to some extent influenced by the standardized and globalized body politics. Therefore, even those who are not displaced from the space of their cities and homelands, are still going through a sexual transformation as inhabitants of the global space, because of the flow of global values. Arjun Appadurai in "Disjunction and Difference in the Global Cultural Economy" claims that the flow of technology and media into developing countries which transfers Western values leads to the detachment of the people of these countries from their cultural values (2003). The Iranian female characters of these works who live in Iranian cities, feel a clash between Muslim radical sexual values and western values which are globalized and perceived as standard. A feeling of dissatisfaction from the present situation is always present in the female characters of the selected works who live in Iranian cities, as a consequence of globalization. Therefore, a new code of behavior and belief is formed among them as a result of the creation of a global space with its globalized values. The idea of rejecting Islamic values in Iran, which is associated with the Islamic revolution and the restricting rules and obligatory dress code of the regime, is a result of the flow of globalization, which promises freedom and leads to a preference for the western lifestyle.

On the other hand, more traditional female characters believe that Islamic and national sexual values and dress code are important to preserve human dignity in women, and protect the Iranian value system against that of the westernized world. They try to stand against the "loss of self" as a result of globalization, and to preserve traditional and religious sexual values as an important part of their cultural identity. So, female beauty and sexuality speak loud in the fight between globalization and localization in the lives of Iranian female characters in the memoirs of Iranian women in the Diaspora.

Another space which plays a very important role in the formation or/and transgression of gendered identity of the female characters in these works is "homeland". The space of homeland is associated with nation, an "imagined community", as Anderson names it (in *Imagined Communities. Reflections on the Origin and Spread of Nationalism*) "because the members of even the smallest nation will never know most of their fellow-members, meet them, or even hear of them, yet in the minds of each lives the image of their communion" (1991).

It is interesting to note how women's sexuality is associated with homeland in these texts. The women are described as having been the preservers of cultural values during centuries. Through this they protect the collective cultural identity which differentiates them and their community from the others (Warner 1998: 3). As transmitters of culture and ideological reproducers of collective symbolisms, women's sexuality plays an important role in preserving the cultural and religious values of the community, and the collective identity of members of Iranian Diaspora. However, for the young generation of diasporic characters who have always lived in the freedom of the host land and wish to belong, it is not an attractive choice to follow the patriarchal cultural values. This mostly leads to conflicts with the parent, even if they used to be progressive and non-traditional before immigration, as the first generation characters mostly becomes more rigid in their traditional values in the diaspora to avoid identity crisis. In some cases the second generation characters experience a return to the cultural values of their nation as adults, because they need to be connected with their homeland as well as the host land.

In an interaction between the traditional cultural identity of the subjects and that of the "Other", their sexual values become dual, hybrid and always in the process of change, as Stuart Hall (Hall 1996) puts it. Therefore, an essentialist definition of Islamic sexual politics is no longer applicable to the sexual identity of Iranian female characters in the Diaspora, as a new version of Islam is being created among them which is full of paradoxes and deviations. However, a puritan view of religion and sexuality in the Diaspora is also reflected in these literary works. Sexual identity defined by religion, as one of the main parts of cultural identity, becomes very important for immigrants who try to preserve their selfhood in the Diaspora.

As reflected in the selected literary and autobiographical works, members of the Diaspora create a parallel community, a third space to feel they belong, are accepted and safe. This is however, constructed on the basis of the subjective images and values which are projected to the whole nation. Belonging to this space is very important for the identity of some of the female characters under discussion. In this space traditional values are observed carefully and even exaggeratedly, to retain a sense of completeness in terms of identity, although aspects of western values are inevitably brought in.

The second focus of this study will be analyzing the effect of bilingualism on the identity formation of the female characters. The generation the characters belong to determines the community they associate themselves with, and their investment in the second language (Norton & Pavlenko 2004). The female characters and the narrators belonging to the first generation of immigrants are expected to stick to the mother tongue and cultural values and transmit them to the next generation.

The female characters and narrators of the first generation are considered the protectors of the value system of the community of Iranians in the Diaspora. However, this causes a lack of interest in language acquisition for these characters. Lack of previous adequate education which facilitates language acquisition, and insufficient contact with the new society and language, are other obstacles that some of the first generation female characters in these works face. However, the female characters of the second generation learn English to integrate into the new society.

The fight to keep one's own identity via language is an important theme in the works in question. The use of English is significant in some of these works as in parts the writers and female characters use Persian grammar in English, or even include Persian words written in the Roman alphabet, which are meaningless to an anglophone reader. This puts the language of the text somewhere between Persian and English, between the language of the characters and that of the English speaking readers. Although English is associated with marginality in several cases, it is also referred as the language of freedom and it gives the subjects a sense of security when they express their inner conflicts in this language. A possible reason which I will discuss in detail in the third chapter is the association of this language with the liberal and modern culture of the hostland and also the proficiency of the characters in this language as they are brought up in the English speaking education system.

The fourth chapter of this research is dedicated to the study of the significance of autobiographical writing for the second generation of Iranian female writers in the Diaspora and the characteristics of their works. Writing helps the female subjects preserve their psychological health through voicing their inner feelings. This makes their writings different from the works of the first generation female memorists of Iranian Diaspora. Amy Motlagh describes the differences between the two generations of Iranian diasporic memoirs of women as follows:

> While first-generation authors are still invested in the depiction of a national story and the possibility of a return to power in the home country, members of the second generation are motivated by different goals. [...] Current memoirists sense the fragmentary nature of the world they live in and simply want to claim that fragmentariness as their own condition. The recent memoirs are no longer intended exclusively to educate Americans about Iran; they are equally invested in teaching themselves and one another about diaspora, a word newly adopted by Iranian Americans to describe their condition (Motlagh 2008: 29).

The intentions and expectations of writing differ between the two generations. The first generation writers are searching for the history and reality of the society of Iran. However, the second generation writers attempt to describe the condition of the characters in the diaspora and their works include the process of remembering and searching for cultural identity.

Here the main themes of the genre created in the diaspora by the second generation female writers will also be studied. As Pnina Werbner points out: "[a[lthough the experience of exile is, in the first instance, personal and individual, long-term diasporas create collective literary genres ... that are uniquely theirs" (Werbner 2000: 17). The genre which is created by Iranian female writers in the Diaspora is unique, but not aimed at the Iranian Diasporic readers (Motlagh 2008: 32).

The effects of the trauma of migration or the catastrophes of revolution, war and so on, which are the main problems of Iranian women in self-exile, form one of the main themes of their writings. Confession through writing is a method of reconciliation with the traumatic past. Shame narratives are also of significance in these works. The narrators express these painful feelings to make peace with themselves and the Other. Besides, the narrators create a dialogue with the

Other and remember their past to achieve a complete image of their identity. Narratives about mother figures are also a dominant part of these autobiographical writings as mother figure plays an important role in the formation of the identity of the female characters. Finally, journalistic style is used in some of the works to express the personal theories of the characters. As Harbord in "Platitudes of Everyday Life" writes:

> Autobiography is never simply about the constitution of a stable, knowable self, even if that is the desire in the writing. The writing of the self involves an engagement with the various cultural resources available, forms which are recognizable to institutions, publishers and audiences. Such conventions do not repress the potential text of the 'self' but constitute its possibilities. The emergence of autobiography in academic work marks a different way of thinking through the relationship of writers to audiences, of negotiating public forms of rhetoric, and of making interventions into the debate about the role of intellectuals. To dismiss it as an intrinsically private activity, signaling a retreat from either public communication or narratives of broader social application, is to miss the point, and to reinstate the tired polarities of public and private, abstract versus embodied knowledge, the political subject versus the narcissist: the ineluctability of othering each other (Harbord 32–33).

In the last chapter of this work, all of the arguments in the chapters of "Space and Gender", "Bilingualism and Gender", and "Writing and Gender" will be summed up. At the end of this research a selected bibliography of the literary works of Iranian female writers in the Diaspora and short biographies of the authors of the case study will be included as appendices.

CHAPTER TWO: SPACE AND GENDER

As narrated in literary productions of female Iranian immigrants, characters' living space and displacement from it, affects their identity. This is particularly significant in case of female characters as their gendered identity and sexuality defines the boundaries between insiders and outsiders of the community. As reflected in the literary productions of Iranian women in the Diaspora the spaces of home, city, and homeland play an important role in the formation of the identity of female characters and displacement from these spaces leads to identity crisis.

Home is the first and most significant space that female characters associate themselves and other female characters with. The space of home, including human interactions taking place in it, time and place, is a refuge from the burden of change and in-betweeness in the Diaspora. In search of a space of belonging, female characters are connected with the space of home. However, they also experience the limitations of the expectations of the community regarding the fixation of female identity as preservers of the space of home. Here I will use the ideas of Julia Kristeva and bell hooks to analyse the association of women to this space and the significance of it for them.

Living in a western city, and the freedom it provides from the limitations in Iranian traditional cities, where traditional sexual norms reign, is a challenging experience for the female characters of the literature of Iranian Diaspora women, and causes sexual, religious and cultural identity crises. However, in these literary works it is not only the changes in the identity of female subjects in the Diaspora, which are discussed. Rather, these works also elaborate on the way the body spaces of female subjects in urban life in Iran are transformed gradually and from generation to generation. In the case of female characters living in Iran, globalized space and globalized sexual identity plays an important role in challenging the traditional understanding of body space and tradition.

The space of homeland, no matter how imaginary it is, creates a sense of belonging for the female characters of these works. As mentioned in the selected autobiographical and literary works, the Iranian diasporic communities directly or indirectly try to protect their collective cultural identities through safeguarding the traditional and religious values. Here, the female characters and their sexual attitudes have a great part as transmitters and protectors of the values of their nation. This, however, restricts female characters in different aspects and leads to detachment from this space for some second generation female characters who feel more attached to the cultural values of the host land, at least as adolescents.

The first space to be considered here is Home. The second space is that of the city, and the comparison between sexual identity of female characters in urban space in Iran and in the western countries. And finally, I will discuss the role of the space of homeland in the identity formation and sexual politics of female characters in the Diaspora.

Home and Gender

Home is not a geographical place, but a space with particular routines and relations in which the subject feels complete in terms of identity. Rapport and Dawson refer to this issue as follow:

> Being 'at home' and being 'homeless' are not matters of movement, of physical space, or of the fluidity of socio-cultural times and places, as such. One is at home when one inhabits a cognitive environment in which one can undertake the routines of daily life and through which one finds one's identity best mediated—and homeless when such a cognitive environment is eschewed (Rapport 1998: 10).

As reflected in the selected autobiographical and literary texts of Iranian women in the diaspora, female characters in the Diaspora often recall the peace and sense of belonging experienced at home. As Kristeva in "Women's Time" claims, home is a place of refuge and origin where identity is absolute and protected (1986: 193). Shadi Ziaei, in her poem "Home", elaborates this issue symbolically.

> Home is not what was said
> Home remains, preserves, stays
> Home home home
> Love is a four-letter word
> Home is a place where chairs and tables
> And words
> Don't stand in your way
> Home is not physics
> It's chemistry
> Home is at the center.
> (Karim 2006: 38)

For the female character in the poem, home is where time is static. It "remains", and "stays" the way it was, and through this, preserves the origin and identity of the character. Also Asayesh writes in her memoir:

> Here in Mashad, the sense of coming home is a powerful one. Caught up in the delights of rediscovery, it is easy to believe in fairy tales, that the world I knew in Iran slumbered like Sleeping Beauty's castle, waiting unchanged for the princess to return. My self-absorption delays the inevitable realization that time has marched on (Asayesh 30).

Kristeva, in the same article, and bell hooks in *Feminist theory, from Margin to Center*, claim that home, as a refuge from history, is often associated with the mother. To retain the unification with self, the subject urges to return home and to the mother who is always "the same" and provides the subject with the illusion of stable selfhood. Asayesh in her work refers to the identification of mother with home and protected identity. Home is where the mother is, no matter whether the home is in Iran or in America.

> I am convulsed by the contradictions of my life, straddling a fissure between two worlds that are immeasurably distant. My mind is always whispering for me to find a more stable spot. Pick one side or the other. Pick one world or the other. I lean sometimes this way, sometimes that. Here in my parents' home, Iran is as tangible as my mother standing at the kitchen table (Asayesh 129).

However, home is for her not only associated with the mother, but also with other female characters, like her aunt, Khaleh Farah.

> Our family is scattered now across two continents. The Gonabad house is empty. Kalateh is gone. And the place I called home in Tehran was razed to the ground years ago. But here on North Gol Street, at Khaleh Farah's house, time has stood still (Asayesh 25).

Jenny Bourne Taylor discusses how the metaphor of exile, and the narratives structured around it, rest on a notion of home, that "home is always the place you come back to, and always from a place of greater complexity" (Bourne 1992: 92-93). In "Recovery" by Nasrin Rahimieh, the female characters are longing for returning home, a space where they used to belong to and exists only in their memories.

> Worlds apart, Ezzat Ammeh and I are dreaming the same impossible dream of returning to the house built by her father and my grandfather. In her rare moments of lucidity, my mother tells me, Ezzat Ammeh asks to be taken home. But she is at home, doctors reassure her, not understanding

that the home she seeks exists now in our collective imagination only.
Our home sits empty, having been sold by my mother when
she could no longer maintain it after my father's death. [...]
Some of the windowpanes are broken; other windows swing
open, making me think back to all those years ago when at
the sign of any down-pour I would become anxious about
windows that might have been left open, worrying that the
torrential rains of Anzali would rot the carved wood of the
panes no workman could replicate.
I wished I had the key to the house and I could let myself
in, shut the windows, repair the damage, and make it ours
again (Karim 2006: 120-121).

Return to home is not possible as time has affected the space and the
relations it facilitates. The character cannot enter the ruined place and
possess it and belong to it. This space is not just a place, it is where
unification with self is possible, and even when the place is demol-
ished, the space survives in the memories of the characters, as they
need somewhere, even imaginary, to belong to. As hooks puts it, at
times of estrangement and alienation "home is no longer just one
place. It is locations. Home is that place which enables and promotes
varied and ever-changing perspectives, a place where one discovers
new ways of seeing reality, frontiers of difference. One confronts and
accepts dispersal and fragmentation as part of the constructions of a
new world order that reveals more fully where we are, who we can become..." (Hooks 1990: 148). The first generation female immigrants of
the selected works have a great attachment to the spaces of home in
Iran, because they have lived a great part of their lives there and have
been also considered the protectors of these spaces which were their
main domain. However, the second generation female characters feel
also connected to their homes in Iran, although they have spent far
less time in these spaces. For them it is the space of reunion with self

too. A good instance of this feeling is where the character "Tara", a second generation female character in Bahrampour's memoir, goes to her old home in Iran which now belongs to others.

> In the spot where Ali and I used to stack up foam couch cushions and sway gleefully between column and wall, a single framed picture of Khomeini stares sternly down. [...] And yet I am dizzy to be here. I return to each room, drinking in its shape, confirming that what I remembered was real... A tightness wells up in my throat—a sadness shot through with elation. Almost nothing of ours remains, and yet I am wildly happy, simply for the fact that this house is still here and I am standing inside it (Bahrampour 251).

However, as Amanda Enayati, in the poem "Native" describes, such a return and unification do not seem possible. Home is used as a geographical metaphor, referring to subject's previous life and the self created in homeland, and has a static tendency as opposed to the dynamic reality of the present surroundings. But the identity of the subject has changed since left and this new self cannot be accepted by the one associated with home.

> The home I left doesn't want me back.
> And if I were to return
> My old home wouldn't unlock
> The gate for me. It wouldn't recognize me.
> My elements changed along the path.
> (Karim 2006: 307)

Besides, she cannot consider her new house abroad a *home*. Home is the realm of stable subjectivity, and as her identity is mobile and unstable, she cannot associate it with the concept of home.

> My new house is no home.
> I realized a bit late—

It has conditions
I do not meet.
Now, I feel like a stranger
All the time.
(Karim 2006: 307)

Due to the restriction of the female domain in Iran women tend to feel closer to each other and establish a sense of collective identity. This forms their perceptions of sexuality and body politics. However, the culture of the host countries tends to reject manifestations of friendly or "sisterly" relations between members of the same sex that are fully acceptable in Iran. A good example of the conflict between the attitudes of Western and Iranian female characters toward this issue is when the character Tara in Bahrampour's memoir expresses her own joys of such innocent bodily contacts, while her American mother is disgusted by them.

> All this touching between women bothered Mama when she was in Iran; She hated the way that after lunch the women would all go off and take naps together, massaging each other's sore legs, braiding each other's hairs, plucking each other's eyebrows and smoothing on ointment afterward. She found those rituals intrusive-especially when coupled with the sexual jokes and insinuations that passed between giggling married women, jokes designed to be tantalizingly inscrutable to unmarried girls who might be listening. But none of this bothers me. I like the slightly bawdy banter among women in my family; I like the touching. It reminds me of the way I used to touch my friends and cousins before the sixth grader in America warned me not to... Now back in it again, I have the sense that it is not just me that they are touching. Running her hands up to my tigh, Leila-khanoum is also touching her own, remembered, self, and that is part of her pleasure. Every girl is a

version of the woman, every woman a model for what the girl will some days be (Bahrampour 342).

Female characters, who are deprived of active presence in public life, seek power in their private lives and at home. Home is a place where female characters govern and make their network of other females. In "Recovery" by Nasrin Rahimieh this phenomena is pictured as follows:

> My happiest memories of our home are of evenings I would accompany my mother downstairs and sit around with the *ammehs.* I can still smell the traditional Gilani straw mats that covered their floors. Sitting cross-legged on the floor with them, my mother would become their confidant and social advisor (Karim 2006: 128).

However, being limited to the space of home, female characters have no knowledge of public life and are only engaged with domestic issues. This is difficult to tolerate for female characters brought up in the Diaspora, or those with a modern western background, as they have got used to more social and cultural spaces and discussions. This is the case of the main female character of Bahrampour's work, Tara, and her American mother.

> I have sometimes thought that the biggest factor keeping me from living in Iran was the alienation I feel when I hear my relatives fervently discussing dresses and dishware; It is the same isolation Mama used to feel, sitting through Tehran tea parties, waiting to get back home to the books and records that connected her to a world that felt like her own (Bahrampour 292).

Another point to mention is the architecture of houses of the characters in Iran. These houses are spacious, with several rooms and gardens. The space allows more communication and contact with nature. Besides, women have a separate place in these houses. Although gender segregated spaces leads to restriction of communication with the other sex, at the same time it provides women with their own territory, where they rule and are free in the way they dress and behave. Returning to this place is not only a great pleasure for the half-Iranian female character "Azadeh" in Moaveni's memoir, but also to her American mother who can free herself from the stress of social responsibilities in the U.S.

> In Tehran that summer, I wasn't the only one unleashed. My mother could barely stay put, flitting from house to house, [...] even when she was at home, sitting down, she was gulping in space-high ceilings, drawing rooms vast enough that I could race a tricycle down from one end to the other—as though her lungs had only been partially breathing the whole time she'd been away. I finally saw Maman, my beautiful, proud, mad mother, laughing gustily, instead of the tight-lipped smile she wore as she chauffeured me around San Jose... (Moaveni 4).

Lack of these spatial potentials and memories and relations associated with them, creates complications in the gender roles of both male and female characters. Male characters have always been the possessors and providers of these spaces for their families in Iran. Not being able to perform this gender role due to financial limitations leads to dissatisfaction and reverses power relations and therefore, the traditional system of the family and community. On the other side, female subjects were always the protectors of this space and when there is no real garden or house to work in and belong to, they also lose their function in the system. Moaveni describes this condition in her memoir as below:

> In California, the absence of gardens seemed the bitterest part of our reconstructed lives. They tried to make do, my grandparents. Their apartment in San Jose, which faced the

> garbage dumpster, had a small, squalid patch of green out front, covered in coarse, dusty ivy. My grandfather, whom we called Agha Joon, patiently cleared it away, and tried to grow *gol-e shamdooni* (geranium). Each day he would water them, determined to make something bloom, to resist letting himself go. My grandmother, fiercely proud, had from the beginning decided on a strategy of not caring; if she could not have her orchards at Farahzad, she didn't want gardens at all (Moaveni 14).

Here the grandfather character tries to make a compromise with the situation and substitute the garden with growing geraniums, typical plants in Iranian houses. However, the grandmother character does not cooperate in this game. She rejects living in an imaginary world. Living in an apartment in San Jose with few plants cannot make her feel at home and belonged.

On the other hand, the female character in *Lipstick Jihad* starts to establish a home in Iran in search of identity and self. She includes some Western and Iranian elements in the decoration, as a metaphor of her double selves. This new home reflects all her dimensions and this makes it a space of peace and belonging.

> I gave up searching for myself, and for what constituted the real Iran, whatever that meant. Instead, I dedicated my days to one task alone: decorating my apartment. [...] The apartment soon became my world—a substitute for the world outside, to which I seemed not to belong, unfit to understand—and so I figured, it might as well look sublime... The objective was to create an interior space where East and West fused with elegance, and the apartment became a canvas on which I could endlessly practice different combinations (Moaveni 112).

As discussed above, the space of home, with the relations it facilitates, is the space of belonging and origin for the female characters of the works mentioned. The subjects urge to return to this space where time has stood still, no matter who this seems impossible. Home is associated with women and above all with mother. Female subjects are expected to preserve this space and spend most of their time here, mostly in the traditional society of Iran, as illustrated in the selected texts. However, besides the restrictions this expectation causes for female subjects, they gain more power in this space as it is their domain.

The other space which affects the gendered identity of female characters in these works is that of cities, both the Iranian ones, as they are experienced or remembered, and the cities in the Diaspora. The characteristics of life in these two spaces, and the comparison between them, shape and change the idea of the female characters of self, sexuality, freedom and religion. Below I will discuss the life in Iranian and western cities and its effects on the identity of the female characters of the case study.

City and Gender

In the literature of Iranian women in the diaspora, there are several references to the undeniable role of city life in Iran and in a western country in the identity formation of female characters. Iranian cities, where the female characters of these works come from and remember, are not mostly vast enough to free the subject from the supervision of others, and social restriction which reigns the lives of the subjects. However, this restriction leads to a security which cannot be found in a modern western city. Besides, life in a traditional Iranian city, as the selected writers picture, favors human relations, which provides the subject with the sense of belonging.

On the other hand, life in western cities provides the female characters with freedom due to anonymity facilitated by the dimension and density. However, insecurity and lack of communication are the harms of this anonymity in western urban life, which leads to identity crisis in some of the female characters in the case study.

Below I will discuss the significance of life in the Iranian cities in the formation and transformation of gendered identity of the female characters of the selected literary works of Iranian women in the Diaspora.

a. Gendered Identity in Iranian Cities

Iranian cities, as reported in these works, are spaces in which religious and moral values reign and people are connected to each other. The urban structure of Iranian cities and the life it facilitates is mostly in favor of interaction among people. Asayesh describes her experience of daily urban life in her home town, when she returns after several years of life in the Diaspora.

> They [close relatives] were all close by, and at night we would walk through the quiet streets of the city on the way home, the children jostling each other playfully, the adults talking and smoking. The street-lights shone on the empty streets, the *Kavir* air was night-cool, and my heart expanded with the joy of being surrounded by family once again (Asayash 90).

As Gelareh Asayesh in *Saffron Sky* narrates, Tehran, the capital of the country, despite resembling most of the capitals of the word in terms of dimension and speed of life, is still a space of intensive communication and traditional values.

> Faith and myth are part of the fabric of daily living. Simple people stop in their tracks to pray when the *muazzin*'s call to prayer drifts from the mosques. Sophisticated people believe in miracles. [...] Such innocence is rare in the country where I make my home. I must bring my daughter halfway across the world to experience it. [...] When a car breaks

down in crowded Tehran, there is no shortage of people stopping to offer advice, water, a ride (Asayesh 178).

According to some of the works under discussion observing the religious rules among female characters are partly due to a longing for the comfort in feeling supported by the social system and an Almighty. Besides, fear of the "Evil Eye" and a will to believe in fate so as to avoid responsibilities are other important reasons of the formation of religious thinking. Another reason, according to some of the works discussed here is, fear of the wrath of God.

Susan Atefeh-Peckham, in her poem "Fariba's Daughters", tries to illustrate the safety provided in following traditional and Islamic rules. She hides under her Grandmother's veil and the world, including the "Revolutionary Guards" (Pasdars), cannot touch her.

> So Grandmother pulled me under her chador,
> wove me into her folds, just me and her under
> cloth so pasdars would leave us alone. Bepau,
> she said, Watch it. And I thought it was fun
> and safe and soft standing against Grandmother's
> lap, seeing from an opening near her hands.
> Perhaps there is some joy in being captive,
> some comfort in knowing we obey.
> (Karim 2006: 202)

As Moaveni writes, some female subjects are not willing to fight against the obligatory dress code. They are too engaged with their daily life and duties to think of their appearance. Their unique identity and self image is lost in the uniformity of gendered roles.

> One's relationship to the veil had been a truly existential question: How important is it to be myself, to have my outside reflect my identity? When faced with this choice, only the true radicals and street warriors chose to flout the dress code. Because it was a fight, they applied war-paint—coats

and coats of makeup—and aggressively risqué cloths. But ordinary women who just wanted to go to work, rather than be Rose Parks through their choice of dress, simply accepted the erasure of their personality through the *roopoosh* uniform (Moaveni 43).

Besides the motive of fear, which makes female subjects follow the rules regarding dress code in the city, some female subjects use Hijab to achieve anonymity and, through this, security and freedom in mobility. Bahrampour in her memoir writes about the experience of the main female character with hijab in Tehran, and the safety it offers through uniformity.

> Government-issue graffiti all over the city proclaim that 'the chador is a woman's freedom', and in a strange way it is. The scarf and raincoat are like a disguise, a protective shield that can make women feel bolder than they otherwise might. I can stare right into this boy's eyes without worrying about a catcall or a hand on my arm; the burden of fending him off has fallen to the state. In any case, it is hardly me he is looking at. Like every woman on the street, I am just a disembodied face to which he can assign hair, breasts, shoulders, and legs. Under this raincoat and scarf, I could be anything he imagines (Bahrampour 267).

However, the comfort of obedience is not the only reason for becoming an observant Muslim. As Tara Bahrampour in her autobiography *To See and See Again* suggests, faith can be a result of a fear of the "Evil Eye" and a will to believe in an unchangeable fate to avoid the heavy burden of responsibility for deeds.

> Within the 'fanaticism', within the willingness to be a martyred and bend to the will of God, lies a simple desire to get from one day to next without interference from the evil eye. It is not prudent to protest, to ask too many questions, to

delve too deeply into the past or the future (Bahrampour 337).

If they believe in fate, people do not need to come to terms with their past or worry about the future and can lead a simpler life. The believers are relieved by finding fate as the reason for their pains and not their or other people's deeds. In Iran with all the catastrophes of revolution and war, this can be a very important drive to believe in fate.

Farnoosh Moshiri suggests another motive for cherishing religious beliefs in "On the Rooftop", the story of a lonely widow whose son is killed after the revolution and her daughter left the country in search of freedom. The character feels death has come to take her, in the form of a little animal or devil, hidden under her veil. As she decides to sleep on the rooftop to die she remembers her past and reveals the reason behind her becoming religious which is the fear of the destructive power of the almighty.

> [S]he smiles and remembers the many summer nights when the kids were little and the house was warm and they all slept on the roof. [...] She didn't believe in God then. Not like now. She didn't even think about God. When she was young she didn't wear a veil, either, not even a scarf. [...] God came in when they left one by one. No, God came in when she began going to the holy shrines to pray for her son. No, God came earlier, when they arrested her son. Yes, He came to her one night in a dream, as a voice, and said, 'You'll need me now. Get up, cover your hair and go to the holy shrine of Ghasem and pray and feed the poor. Go on foot if you want your son to get released' (Karim 2006: 156-157).

Tara Bahrampour in her autobiography *To See and See Again* suggests that practicing religion is mostly a social experience for the female characters in the Iranian city pictured in the work, who are restricted in their access to public life.

> For Aziz, going to the mosque was more of a social event than a spiritual one. She would walk over to the mosque, talk a little with the other women, and come home furious about the mullah's hour-long discussion about 'which hand to eat with and which hand to wipe yourself with.' Ranting about how they were making a fool of her, she would swear that she wasn't going back anymore, but she always did (Bahrampour 16).

Besides religious spaces, female characters living in the Iranian cities of these works are allowed to have free social presence in women-only places like gyms. In her memoir, Moaveni reflects the experience of the main female character in a gym in Tehran as follows:

> Many of the women there were obviously the mistresses of these rich men because they were too young, breathtakingly beautiful, and middle class to afford the class otherwise. [...] for some reasons they hated me. [T]hey clearly believed I rushed home every day to be fed sugar dusted grapes and fanned with a palm frond, and they tortured me with incessant, niggling assertions of their authority over the world of the gym. It seemed the less power women had in the world outside, the more they sought to flex their influence in the small universe inside (Moaveni 153).

It is in such spaces where women have freedom in dress code and behavior and can be free in the absence of men. Here women have power and try to preserve it through making territories and rules. The female character "Azadeh" who has been living in America for many years and does not know the power relations of such spaces is, therefore, considered an outsider here.

However, not all the Iranian cities in these works are the same in terms of restricting women in accessing public places, and leaving them only religious or women-only spaces in the city. Firouzeh Dumas describes Abadan, the home town of the main female character, as a city providing more opportunities for social interactions for women, owing to the remainders of British planning and mentality. She mentions these exceptions as she is aware of the restricting norms in other Iranian cities.

> By the time I was born in Abadan in 1965, there was no longer a large British population in town. A few foreigners remained, all employed by the operating companies. Iran was finally reaping most of the profits from its own oil. In the absence of the British, the residents of Abadan benefited from a city built by thoughtful British planners. We had swimming pools, clubhouses, and very orderly housing developments. My hometown looked different from any other Iranian city (Dumas 85).

Even in Tehran of the childhood of the female character in "Becoming a Woman" by Elham Gheytanchi, where Islam and patriarchy limit women in their mobility and behavior in the public, there are zones in which female characters have more freedom, at least as children. The Jamalzadeh neighborhood in central Tehran is where Christians, Jews, Zoroastrians and Muslims live together. The freedom other religions offer women affects the mentality of Muslim families and girls are allowed to participate in social life. However, becoming a woman decreases her public presence and the community imposes gender roles on the subject.

> I grew up and became a woman in Jamalzadeh *koucheh* (alley) in Tehran. [...] Our neighbors were Zoroastrians, Christians, Muslims, and Jews. It was only later that I found out our street was a unique place in Tehran. As a kid, we spent most of our time playing in the street. [...] It was in the au-

tumn of 1979, just as the revolution was taking place, that I
became a woman. [...] I really did have two small nuts on
my chest. My mother looked at me and said: 'I told you ...
no more football. And you shouldn't run in the street so
much. Try to act like a woman.' [...] Acting like a woman, I
gradually found out, indeed meant severe limitations, less
presence in public, and definitely no running like I used to.
Kia, however, was becoming a man. Contrary to my experience, his space only widened. [...] Later that year, I had to
wear *hijab* to go to school. My space shrunk even more ...
(Karim 2006: 180-181).

Some Iranian female characters of these works, living in Iranian cities,
feel a clash between Muslim radical sexual values and western values
which are globalized and perceived as standard. The global values are
associated with freedom and joy, could result in the rejection of Islamic and traditional values, or creation of an in-between dress code
and system of behavior in Iranian urban spaces. Arjun Appadurai in
"Disjunction and Difference in the Global Cultural Economy" claims
that due to the flow of technology and media into developing countries, which transfer Western values, people in such countries experience a detachment from their own cultural values (2003). The clash
between Muslim radical values and globalized ones affects urban lives
of Iranian female characters of the mentioned works in Iranian cities.
In Bahrampour's memoir, the main female character, narrates the ideas
of Roya, a female subject living in Tehran, regarding this issue.

Roya, too, points out that young people, forced indoors by
the Islamic regulations, are doing things their parents' generation never dreamed of. The attempt to eradicate Western
culture seems to have produced a virulent resistant strain.
Young people who want to be 'Western' hook up illegal
satellite dishes and watch American shows like *Beverly Hills
90210*, *Dallas*, and *Baywatch*. Since many of those watching

have no other picture of what America is like, They assume
from watching the TV shows that all Americans have a lot
of sex with the people they barely know. Striving to be like
Americans, they do their best to follow suit (Bahrampour
267).

Tehran is a quite westernized city in its appearance, as Bahrampour
describes. However, the regulations governing the city are Islamic and
traditional, including gender segregation. This paradox, however, does
not keep the subject from having secret relationships with the other
sex.

On a Thursday night, the start of the Iranian weekend, the
Golestan Mall is buzzing with activity. Brightly lit, ultra-
modern shop windows display imported jeans, hiking
shows, perfumes, and snowboards. A jewelry shop glitters
with Italian bracelets and swiss watches; a stationary store
offers Hemingway paperbacks in English. As we window
shop, Sima points at the parade of young people strolling
back and forth, grazing each other's shoulders. 'Sit and
watch for a half hour and you'll notice things,' she says.
'See that group of boys pretending to talk to each other?
Well, they're really talking to that group of girls behind
them' (Bahrampour 271).

The concept of beauty is also changed due to the globalization of body
aesthetics. Female characters try to adjust themselves to the new
standards through plastic surgery and changes made in their body
spaces. In "If You Change Your Nose" Leyla Momeny mentions the importance of nose surgery for the mother and sister, as they believe this
can change their destiny. However, the narrator who is brought up in
the diaspora does not share this idea.

if you change your nose,
you change your destiny

my mother's changed hers twice
my sister, once
1 am quietly planning an escape
[...]
but I prefer
the beauty of Ugliness,
and in between
the post-surgery and celebration, I rush back and forth
from these two, three, or four worlds.
(Karim 2006: 161-162)

Also Dumas writes of the importance of a plastic surgery for Iranian women as a means of guaranteeing their future marriage: one of the most important issues in the life of women. Here one sees that the globalized standards of beauty are being observed although the community is still traditional in its criteria for a successful woman.

> In Iranian culture, a woman's nose is much more than a breathing device; it is her destiny. A girl with an ugly nose learns early on to dream of one thing only—a skilled plastic surgeon.
> Only the poorest families do not intervene to correct nature's nasal missteps. No amount of charm, talent, or intelligence can make a girl overcome an ugly nose; it simply must be fixed (Dumas 161).

Besides, the problematization of the aesthetics of body, sexuality is problematized in Tehran after the Revolution due to the excessive gender segregation in urban life according to the female narrator in Moaveni's memoir. Illegalization of relationships among the sexes before marriage has led to underground relations. In the selected literary and autobiographical works such relationships are described as a result of curiosity about love and sex, which is introduced to female characters living in Islamic Tehran through globalization.

Though highly traditional spheres of Iranian society had socialized along gender lines—with men and women in separate rooms, or separate sides of the room, at parties—platonic interaction and friendship had been ordinary among secular middle-class and upper-class Iranians. The revolution reversed this. It threw up obstacles everywhere to casual coexistence between the sexes: segregated elementary schools and university classes, segregated buses, segregated restaurant lines, segregated passport offices.

> Separated most of the hours of the day, young people became mysterious to each other, familiar but alien. [...] Being together involved sneaking away, into the dark corners of public parks, into the woods in the Alborz Mountains, into each other's empty houses (Moaveni 190).

However, not all the female characters living in Iranian cities believe that application of globalized values in Iranian urban spaces is a sign of progress. More traditional female characters believe that Islamic and traditional sexual values and dress code are important to preserve human dignity in women, and protect the Iranian value system against that of the westernized world. The narrator of Moaveni's memoir also refers to some more traditional women who believe "make up is meant to mimic how women look when they are aroused". They try to stand against the "loss of self" as a result of globalization, and to preserve traditional and religious sexual values in social life as a key part of their identity. These believe that Islamic values and dress code are important to preserve human dignity in women and protect the value system of the country against that of the westernized world. Therefore, female beauty and sexuality play an important role in the fight between globalization and localization in the urban lives of Iranian female characters in the memoirs of Iranian women in the Diaspora.

Another harm of Islamization of the urban life in Iran, which Azadeh Moaveni in *Lipstick Jihad* refers to, is the depression of the first generation of female characters living in Iranian cities after the revolution. They have to observe the rigid Islamic regulations and dress code, instead of enjoying the freedom and facilities of globalized urban life.

> The general stressors of Tehran life—toxic smog, traffic jam, fundamentalist theocracy inflation, unemployment—together with the special burden of the veil made Iranian life particularly wearisome for women, who were depressed in large numbers. The depression had a major, physical component, in that it was compounded by the clothing regulations of the regime. [...] Why do your hair if it's going to be covered all day? Why watch your figure if it gets lost in the folds of a cloak? [...] As a result, women often found the find line between a practical approach to Islamic Republic grooming and slovenliness blurred. Before you knew it, you had devolved into a sloppy version of yourself [...] (Moaveni 156-157).

Islamic dress code, which is to be observed in public urban spaces in Iran, has also caused a sense of isolation of female characters of the first generation after the revolution, according to the main female character of Moaveni's work. This generation, which has experienced freedom before the Islamic revolution, does not want to accept the new limitations and prefers to remain in private spaces, far from urban life and its regulations.

> They preferred to cloister in the company of old friends, in worlds carefully constructed to turn inwards, and deflect the reality of the present as much as possible. That could mean wearing just one *manteau* for years, staying inside all day endlessly redecorating apartments (Moaveni 160).

However, the female subjects of the second generation are not willing to deprive themselves of the joys of social life, although the traditional regulations and dress code reign the city. They transform hijab as a defense method against the obligatory dress code, which limits them in mobility and leads to isolation, anonymity and sloppiness. This makes them in some cases even too pre-occupied with their body space.

> They [young women living in Iran] were more inclined to exploit the fresh permissiveness in the dress code and quickly adapted to the new reality of being able to wear whatever they wanted, as long as it skimmed their upper thighs. Since they were coming of age in a roopoosh that revealed, instead of cloaked, they had the dubious privilege of becoming preoccupied with body image. The fret of their mother's generation ('Am I letting myself go under this tent?') was replaced with a more universal, modern concern ('Is my butt too big?'). Perhaps in its own strange way, this counted as progress (Moaveni 156-157).

This generation lives an underground life. There is a globalized Tehran living in heart of the traditional city. The young female subjects try to reconcile the Islamic regulations with their modern needs. In this regard Moaveni writes:

> Everywhere, it seemed, there were barriers. Of thought and behavior, of places and time. And most dizzying of all, a culture of transgression that could only be learned through firsthand experience. For women, there were eternal limits on dress and comportment, but they could be flouted easily —in the right neighborhood, at the right time of the day or month, in the right way. Young couples also faced endless prohibitions, but these too could be circumvented, with the right verbal pretexts, at the right times, in the right places (Moaveni 55).

Female characters hold fashion shows in gender segregated Tehran with obligatory Islamic dress code, manifesting the transformation of hijab, and symbolically, the value system. They try to change the situation gradually towards globalization, without radical actions or isolating themselves.

> One part of me shivered with delight at the thought of a fashion show in the Islamic Republic. A public event dedicated to the expression and aesthetic of femininity, in a place so hostile to all things feminine and physical. Another part of me registered disappointment, because a regime-sanctioned cat-walk signaled a societal entrenchment of the veil. [...] But I reminded myself that women's absorption in their physical appearance, in itself, communicated a powerful message. It meant they were not forfeiting their bodies, their right to express themselves, enshrined in the seemingly superficial but deeply symbolic matter of outer garb (Moaveni 161).

As discussed above, life in the Iranian urban spaces play an important role in the identity formation of female characters of the selected literary works of Iranian women in the diaspora. In these spaces traditional and religious values are dominant. This provides the female subjects with security but at the same time limits their freedom in mobility, sexuality and dress code. The clash between global values and Muslim ones leads to the creation of an underground life which facilitates more freedom for the female subjects but includes risks of sexual victimization too.

Below the different aspects of life in Western urban spaces and its effect on the gendered identity of Iranian female characters in the Diaspora, as reflected in the sources studied here, will be analyzed.

b. Western Cities and Gendered Identity

Gendered identity cannot be formed without tradition and a supportive social system. That is why the identity and values of the female subjects in the mentioned works change when they are displaced from the religious/traditional social system of Iranian urban spaces. Modern

Western cities make civic freedom uniquely possible due to their density and anonymity it provides. This freedom, however, has dangers of victimization, prostitution and problematization of sexuality for female citizens according to Pamela K. Gilbert in "Sex and the Modern City", where she is writing about the condition of female characters in English novels of 19th century, coming from margins of rural life to the center of urbanity. It is a challenge for some Iranian female characters of these literary works and autobiographies to protect themselves against the harms of this freedom. Asayesh in the same work writes:

> [I]n America childhood seemed to end early, to be replaced by a cultivated cynicism that masked both vulnerability and immaturity. I was still a child, with a child's joy in simple pleasures and a secret delight in the safety of rules and restrictions. Going to high school in America felt like a violation of my childhood, an abrupt and painful loss of innocence (Asayash 110).

However, Iranian Muslim tradition of chastity is considered as a defense method against these dangers, although religion and tradition have patriarchal tendencies of repressing female sexuality. Leyla Momeny's "Persian Princess Insania" refers to this issue as follows:

> The men in my family
> Never learnt how to cry
> They built cities over their own dreams
> Engineers of a keener reason
> Rolex-wristed namesakes holding my hand,
> Nihilist-hedonist patriarchs taught me to fly!
> My chastity, preserved.
> (Karim 2006: 41-42)

PAZ in "1979" tells the story of a young Iranian girl living in America and benefiting from the freedom to follow her lesbian needs. She does not know that lesbianism is a taboo and great sin in Iranian Islam and tradition. When her father learns about the lesbian tendencies of the daughter he starts his religious education

> The first sermons I got from dad as he tucked me into bed was about the golden castle that was being built for me in heaven. God's angels were busily building a castle for me in heaven out of gold bricks. Every time I had good thoughts or did good deeds, they would add a golden brick to my future home in the sky. But every time I had bad thoughts or did bad deeds, they would take five bricks away. [...] I did the math and realized that I had better get my act 'straight' or I would be homeless by the time I died and went to heaven (Karim 2006: 69-70).

The fear of "homelessness" as a result of bad deeds is so great that the girl decides to act "straight" and follow the religious rules and definitions of bad and good. As Wilson argues, women in western visions of the metropolis have seemed to represent disorder. City is a space of uncontrolled and chaotic sexuality, and the rigid control of women in cities is necessary to avoid this danger (Wilson 1991: 157). Fatima Mernissi in *Beyond the Veil: Male-Female Dynamics in Modern Muslim Society* refers to the restrictions male Muslim subjects impose on female Muslim subjects in their access to public spaces. She writes: "Since women are considered by Allah to be a destructive element, they are to be spatially confined and excluded from matters other than those of the family. Female access to non-domestic space is put under the control of males" (Mernissi 19). Freeman believes that restricting female mobility in the society are common in all patriarchal communities: "In the 'East' and the 'West' alike, fears and anxieties concerning women's freedom and emancipation have been related to a community's desire to control women's sexuality and to ensure their 'purity'. This intersection between morality and mobility is one of many factors that shape women's access to and experiences of migration and movement at different scales" (Freeman 2005: 150). Besides, Observing traditional values and

Islamic dress code and sexual politics provides the subjects with a sense of safety. As Tonkiss puts it:

> One of the starkest forms in which gender difference and gender inequality appear in the city is in the geography of violence against women. Even in urban contexts where cultural or legal dictates do not deny women full access to public spaces, it can be argued that many women's perceptions and use of urban space are restricted by logics of sexual dominance and fear (Tonkiss 2005: 95).

Asayesh refers to the prohibition for female characters to access to some urban spaces in American cities, because such spaces were not controllable by the community. Representatives of patriarchal value system of the community feared that Iranian female characters would use their freedom and betray the traditional religious values of the community or encounter the dangers of sexual abuse:

> I was not allowed to 'date' boys. Dating was a wholly foreign concept to me, because it removed young people from the family context that reigned supreme in Iran. In Westernized Tehran, we may have gone to a movie with a boy, but we lived our lives in a context shaped by adults. Here, teenagers seemed to live in their own parallel universe in which they made the rules. To me, it looked like anarchy. I had no interest in trading my world for theirs. But if by some fluke some boy someday asked me to go to Purdy's, the teenage disco on Franklin Street that my classmates raved about, I wanted to be able to say yes (Asayesh 117).

Despite the strong expectation of the communities of Iranians in the diaspora from the female characters to observe the Iranian cultural values, religious and traditional values of these characters are transgressed in Western cities. "[R]eligious identities", writes R. Stephen Warner in "Immigration and Religious Communities in the United

States", "often (but not always) mean more to [individuals] away from home, in their Diaspora, than they did before, and those identities undergo more or less modification as the years pass" (1998: 3). A very good example of this is found in Leyla Dowlatshahi's "Stones in the Garden". In this story, Khaleh Farah, her daughter Shada, a beautiful and religious girl, and her niece Roya, who is 16 years old and is always compared to Shada as she is a good religious girl, are living in a refugee asylum in Germany. They are going to a mosque for prayer and Roya is being teased for not caring about prayer time. They have just received a refugee food box containing pork, which is religiously prohibited. Khaleh Farah takes the pork to the flat of a neighbor, whose sons are playing outside, and who appears to be a prostitute.

> Khaleh Farah placed the box next to him, and then she and the two girls walked past the security camera and out the heavy front door. Outside, Shada turned back to look in at Yuri and Isak sitting on the bench.
> 'It is a shame ... the way she carries on ... leaving those boys alone all day!' began Shada angrily.
> 'What can we do? It is none of our business if she wants to sell herself. She must deal with Allah', replied Khaleh Farah.
> 'Yes, Maman. You are right. Her fate is up to Allah', Shada said quietly. 'Come. Let's go.'
> They walked into the warming fall morning ... *Did I imagine it? S*he [Roya] thought. She hurried to follow Khaleh Farah and Shada into the mosque (Karim 2006: 252).

It is significant that the conservative, religious aunt, who cannot accept even a late prayer from her daughter and niece, is flexible in her relations with foreign women and even helps them, although she does not approve their deeds. This paradox in religious identity is a result of living in the western city with its freedom and plurality.

As Barbara Metcalf in *Making Muslim Space in North America and Europe* puts it, "[t]he sense of contrast—contrast with a past or contrast with the rest of society—is at the heart of a self-consciousness that shapes religious style" (1996: 7). And as Vertovec in *Transnationalism* explains, the self-consciousness of migrant minorities due to a condition of pluralism relates to, and may in certain ways overlap with, the identity dynamics associated with the condition of Diaspora (2009: 141). In other words, they may be diasporic subjects who prefer to identify with the "other", to belong and to be accepted as citizens. This includes rejecting the traditional religion and cultural beliefs, which is a recurrent theme in the poems of the second generation of Iranian women in the Diaspora, as e.g. in "Bad" by Sanaz Banu Nikaein:

> I am bad:
> To hold my lover's hand in public
> enjoy watching him sleep
> In my bed
> Before marriage
> Bad [...]
> Tradition disowns me as a member
> I disown the culture as a follower
> Still the eyes of my community watch my every move
> (Karim 2006: 196).

Another problem which female characters face, as reflected in the poetry of Iranian women in the Diaspora, is the urban planning of western city which makes human relations difficult due to its population density. On the contrary, the urban structure of Iranian cities and the life it facilitates are mostly in favor of interaction among people. In "Raw walnuts" Negin Neghabat pictures this contrast:

> People's smiles and compliments there, in my first country,
> stood in such massive contrast to the cold, harsh treatment
> I received in the country that eventually became my second
> home—Germany (Karim 2006: 133).

Besides, Susan Atefat-Peckham in "Sestinelle for Travelers", uses the metaphor of a cold unknown city where she has always lived to imply lack of communication and detachment.

> These are the alleys, ravines, side streets travelled all our
> lives,
> Shadows
> That hang the sun at our back, the canopy of telephone
> wire
> And wings.
> We are bound for the silence. Unknown roads
> Curve through the heat, where metal clamps of trucks cor-
> rode
> And life is a falling turquoise pendant flipping from an old,
> gold string
> Down the path of this blue world the traveler knows
> (Karim 2006: 237-238).

Social interaction and communication in urban life is one of the great needs of the main female subject of Bahrampour's word, as she has got used to it in Iranian cities. However, as it is not possible for her to return to these spaces, she tries to substitute the warm human relations in Iranian cities with those in New York. Unlike California, where urban planning provides people with more privacy and distance from others, New York and Tehran are spaces of communication. People in New York look out for each other like Tehranis. Even prying in other's affairs is common in these cities. However, the subject finds it positive and a sign of people caring for each other. She writes:

> I think that on some level, I moved to New York because it reminded me of Tehran. I liked the man who held the subway door open so a stranger could race down the stairs and make it onto the train. I liked the officious woman behind me in the deli checkout line who told me that everyone was using olive oil now at the table instead of butter. New York-

ers were different from Californians, who don't take trains and who have so much room in supermarket aisles that no one needs to talk to anyone else. New Yorkers pried into each other's affairs and looked out for each other in the same way Iranians did (Bahrampour 206).

Although communication and human relations in western cities are generally far less intensive than in Iranian ones, some female characters in Dumas's work find the condition more critical after the Iranian revolution and hostage crisis. The subjects migrating to American cities after this event faced more restriction in their access to urban life as people's aggressive behavior left them with less security in the cities.

> When my parents and I get together today, we often talk about our first year in America. Even though thirty years have passed, our memories have not faded. We remember the kindness more than ever, knowing that our relatives who immigrated to this country after the Iranian Revolution did not encounter the same America. They saw Americans who had bumper stickers on their cars that read 'Iranians: Go Home' or 'We Play Cowboys and Iranians'. The Americans they met rarely invited them to their houses. These Americans felt that they knew all about Iran and its people, and they had no questions, just opinions. My relatives did not think Americans were very kind (Dumas 36).

Moaveni also refers to the changes which the marginalization of Iranian subjects in Los Angeles after the hostage crisis has caused in their lives and identity. Some have decided to integrate completely in the American society and life style, and others with less academic background have invested in the creation of a parallel city of their own in Los Angeles, where they can live a prosperous urban life.

The hostage crisis had forever stained our image in the American psyche, and slowly I saw how this shaped so much of what we did and strove for as immigrants... Iranians coped with this oppressive legacy in various ways. Some, like parts of my family, willed it away by losing any trace of Persian accent, and becoming so professionally successful that they entered a stratum of American society sophisticated enough to understand and appreciate their presence and contribution. Some, nearly a million in fact, sought strength in numbers and founded a colony in Los Angeles. They seemed unfazed by their growing reputation for vulgarity and obsession with image; better to be associated with a penchant for BMWs than revolutionary Islam, they figured (Moaveni 25).

Bahrampour refers to this Iranian city in heart of Los Angeles as Tehrangeles. However, to her, it does not resemble the Tehran of her memories. The female characters of this new space are obsessed with money and appearance, and are difficult to communicate with. The American urban life style and the fear of inferiorization has (trans-) formed their identity in the Diaspora. The public space of café does not resemble the ones in Tehran with the simple human relations they are associated with.

Westwood is getting so full of Iranian that they've given it a nickname, 'Tehrangeles'. I don't like it. I don't like the clumps of Iranian girls dressed in Gloria Vanderbilt jeans, holding little black purses with gold-chain straps, and I don't like the cafe, which is overpriced and full of dressed-up Iranians with nothing better to do in the middle of the day than sit on wrought-iron chairs and drink tea... I know that this is not like the real Iran. In the real Iran this would be a pastry shop, and a scruffy-faced man in a blue tunic would shovel fresh raisin cookies into a box and let Sufi put

her finger on the knot of the string when he tied it
(Bahrampour 150).

As discussed above, life in the Western cities provides female characters of the selected literary works of Iranian women in the Diaspora
with freedom which includes risks of victimization. Besides, this freedom detaches some of the female characters of second generation from
traditional values, which is a threat to the collective identity of the
community of Iranians in the diaspora. Another aspect of life in Western cities is lack of communication due to the dimensions of the city
and the speed of life.

Besides the impact of life in western cities on gendered identity and
sexual politics of female characters in these works, displacement from
the public space of the homeland is also of great significance, as I will
discuss below.

Homeland and Gender

In the literature of Iranian women in the Diaspora there are several
references to the geographical characteristics of the homeland and the
relationships and values governing it, which add different dimensions
of the space of homeland. The characters have a sense of attachment to
this space to ease the pain of marginalization and discrimination in the
diaspora. The authors make a utopia out of the homeland through
memory and imagination to "de-stress themselves from the distress of
not belonging by living in an imaginary world that is magical, poetic,
fable-like", as Nandini Sahu discusses in her instruction to *The Post-
Colonial Space: Writing the Self and the Nation* (2007: xxi). This act of
making a fable-like image of the nation covers not only cultural spaces,
but also geographical spaces. And even the boundary between cultural
and geographical are blurred, as space is always subjectively perceived
(Rose 58). This means that the character refers to any cultural and natural characteristic of the home land as a part of national cultural iden-

tity of the community and an anchor to keep the diasporic characters safe from loss of identity. Asayesh writes:

> I dreamed not only of the faces of those I loved but of the land. My hunger for the desert and mountains and sea was tangible, like a child's longing for her mother's embrace. We are all a product of our physical geography; it is as if the contours of earth and water and leaf that fill our eyes during childhood create a corresponding landscape of the mind. It lingers dormant within us, an inner vision seeking completion in outer reality (Asayesh 23).

By being related to a homeland, one benefits a sense of belonging. The subject can be identified and differentiated by being associated with a specific nation. Homi Bhabha in "Dissemi-Nation: Time, Narrative, and the Margins of the Modern Nation" speaks movingly of the gathering of scattered peoples: "The nation fills the void left in the uprooting of communities and kin, and turns that loss into the language of metaphor" (1994:139). Asayesh writes

> For months I keep the dust of Iran in my shoes, and it makes me miserable.
> Gradually I let go. I channel my anguish into trying to infuse some Iranianness into days that feel almost totally American. I buy Iranian tapes. I start praying again, for a time. I renew my attempts to teach Neil Farsi. It is a pattern that will become familiar in the course of subsequent trips to Iran.
> One day I wake up and there is joy to life again (Asayesh 65).

In many cases, the female characters of the selected sources are required by the community to retain Iranian cultural values and the traditional image so that the collective identity of the community is not disturbed. Anthias & Yuval-Davis, in *Racialized Boundaries: Race, Nation, Gender, Colour and Class and the Anti-Racist Struggle* claim that:

> Women and their sexualities emerge as significant markers and perpetuators of these [insider/outsider] boundaries, and by extension as sources and sites for transgressing the said boundaries. Moreover, they point to at least three elements that bring out central aspects in the lineaments between the constructions of nations, ethnicities and boundary formation in and through the control of the feminine body. Namely: i) as biological producers of the 'collective' [race/nation/ethnic group]; ii) as boundary markers and therefore reproducers of these boundaries; iii) as transmitters of culture and the ideological reproduction of collective symbolisms (1993: 113).

Therefore, it is not surprising that silence in confrontation with undesirable aspects of the patriarchal society and fixation to cultural values of the nation are considered a part of women's duty in Iranian Diaspora, to protect the cultural identity, as Tara Fatemi refers to in her poem "Women's Duty".

> No word could fly out and hum bee-stings
> Into our tender ears, darling. Stitches
> So even and fine they were invisible.
> Months later I got too close
> To the mirror, jumped back from
> Langling lipthreads and screamed
> To ears whose drums had closed
> From lack of use
> (Karim 2006: 145).

Massey notes that in insisting on "bounded" definitions of space or place which are defined against an Other, one might argue that, according to the object relations theory, "security of boundaries, the requirement for such a defensive and counter-positional definition of identity, is culturally masculine" (1994: 7). As Asayesh writes in her memoir, this is the father who expects the daughters to preserve their Iranian cultural identity through repressing their sexuality.

> Baba would try to impress on us two things: one, the importance of going back to Iran; and two, the importance of retaining our identity. This latter topic was littered with references to the iniquities of Western culture. Baba told us early and often that there is only one thing American boys want from girls: bed. His face was twisted in distaste as he said this, for he is the product of a puritanical culture. Like most parents, he was also acutely uncomfortable discussing sex with his daughters. In Iran, it would not have been an issue. But now my sister and I were living in a moral jungle, rampant with sex, drugs, and alcohol (Asayesh 116).

There is a deeply ingrained "depiction of the homeland as the female body whose violation by foreigners requires its citizens and allies to rush to her defense" (Parker *et al.* 1992: 6). I believe that this analogy is also applicable to the cultural values associated with the country which should be protected, like the honor of a woman. To illustrate this, one could cite "Waiting for Ulysses" by Laleh Khalili. In this poem she portrays the country and its culture as a woman, Penelope, waiting for her lover, Ulysses, who is in exile. She has to protect herself against suitors and longs to be cared and protected by Ulysses. Khalili has created this image to suggest that Iran and Iranianness after the revolution are endangered and those who could protect the space of homeland have left it:

> Penelope in darkness
> Unraveled
> Awaiting the end of all exile
> Groves of tangerine and *naranj* rotten on the branches
> And the algaed imperturbability of lonely reflecting pools
> In forgotten courtyards (Karim 2006: 148).

The creation of an "Imaginary Homeland" is another result of displacement from the home land. According to Salman Rushdie (1992), after migration subjects make a static and utopia-like image of homeland and its value system and live with it. This gives them a feeling of being in their "real" home, a sense of completeness in terms of identity. Besides, in his study of the rise and expansion of nations and nationalism, *Imagined Communities*, Anderson (1991: 12) notes that an imagined community is different from an actual community because it is not (and cannot be) based on everyday face-to-face interaction between its members. Instead, members hold in their minds a mental image of their affinity. Bahrampour writes about this image of nation and homeland which is frozen in memories and mystified:

> People might tell me stories about what Iran was really like, but they were not talking about 'my' Iran. We had left at the end of my childhood, and like childhood it had frozen in my mind into a mythical land. Once we landed in America, I lost the power to separate Iran from my memories of what it had been (Bahrampour 203).

The native-aliens or second generation of Iranians in the diaspora have nostalgia for the homeland and suffer from identity problems too, although they have not lived in Iran. Their knowledge of homeland comes from memories of childhood trips, the stories of parents about their magic life in Iran, and the advertisements in the media. This image is collective and the subject who needs to have a clearer picture of life in the space of homeland needs to travel back and experience it herself. "Iranian" is the only sense of national cultural identity in these works. The first generation subjects who are brought up in Iran are so attached to their homeland that consider themselves as diasporic characters and do not have a sense of belonging in their new surroundings. The second generation female subjects, although interested in melding in the new society as adolescents, find Iranianness a great part of their identity as adults. To them happiness and hope are feelings left behind in the homeland. Moaveni refers to this condition as so:

> Once I discovered the joys of my own private Iranianness, I was reluctant to dilute it with anything reminiscent of the years of adolescent conflict. Growing up Iranian in America had been arduous and awkward. We had little consciousness of assimilation, because we were in denial of our permanence in America. My mother always made this perfectly clear. We are *not* immigrants. Immigrants come on boats. We came on planes. We were émigrés, exiles, mentally still in between. In such an atmosphere, I had never felt American at all, and so I dispensed altogether with the idea of being a hyphened American. When people asked me where I was from, I smiled tightly and said, 'Iran'. Full stop. Shoulders pulled back. Defensive. Knowing perfectly well that the answer was misleading, but too exhilarated by the fresh feelings of pride and coherence to care. In my own mind, I was just plain Iranian; even though the second I opened my mouth, my sentences bubbled with those unconscious 'likes', and anyone could tell that California figured in the story. An unintended consequence of this was that I actually began believing it. Soon I came to assume, with reckless confidence, that since I was Iranian, I would feel at home in the one place I was meant to belong—Iran (Moaveni 28).

In the memoirs and autobiographical writings of the second generation female authors is a return to Iran and home a main theme. In Moaveni's memoir the narrator needs to refresh her idea of the homeland and is in the quest of her understanding of "Iran" and not the one built upon the stories of family members or media. Through this, however, the character is in search of her identity too.

> What I wanted, though I chose not to admit it to myself, was to figure out my relationship to this other country, to Iran. Originating from a troubled country, but growing up outside it, came with many complications. Worst of all, at least on a personal level, was that you grew up assuming everything about you was related to that place, but you never got to test that out, since the place was unstable and sort of dangerous, and you never actually went there. You spend a lot of time watching movies about the place, crying in dark theaters, and feeling sad for your poor country. Most of that time, you were actually feeling sorry for yourself, but since your country was legitimately in serious trouble, you didn't realize it. And since it was so much easier and romantic to lament a distant place than the day-to-day crappy messes of your own life, it could take a very long time to figure it all out.
>
> That, really, was why I wanted to go to Iran. To see whether the ties that bound me were real, or flimsy threads of inherited nostalgia. The momentum grew inside me, tentative and slow, but I called it by other names, unprepared to begin fiddling with the rubik's cube of my identity (Moaveni 32-33).

Also Asayesh refers to the return to her homeland as a means of reunion with Iranian cultural identity.

> With that first trip back, I began the long, slow road toward resurrecting a buried self. And vowed I would never suffer that inner shriveling of an isolated core, the immigrant's small death, again (Asayesh 113).

However, the female character Shahrzad in Bahrampour's memoir finds the risk of shattering her memories and the concept of the "homeland" in traveling to Iran. Shahrzad says:

> I had a friend who went back [...] she was so excited. But she said Iran was so different she could not recognize it. All her memories were shattered [...] Don't you see? I can't risk having my memories shattered (Bahrampour 194).

Food also plays an important role in the preservation of the cultural identity of the subjects. I would argue that this is firstly because of its being an inseparable part of the rituals and secondly due to its being specific to the people and geography associated with the space of homeland. In "Ode to Eggplant" Persis M. Karim refers to the role of food in bringing people together

> And the heat from which you are born
> is the heat you unleash
> in the slow simmer of sauce and stew that
> gathers people to an intimate table
> (Karim 2006: 139).

 In "Raw Walnut" by Negin Neghabat the narrator speaks of the particular way of preparation of walnut, specific to Iranians. The taste of the raw walnut is associated with homeland and belonging.

> Crack the hard shell of walnuts, throw the shell away and placethe walnuts in a jar of water. Change the water every few hours, and repeat this for several days. Eventually, the thin brown skin gets soft and can be peeled off easily. With only the bare, white part of the walnut remaining, add some salt, and try tasting the 'raw walnut'. For me, this taste brings back memories of a time when I still had a nation and the sense of belonging (Karim 2006: 133).

However, there is a love-hate relationship among some of the female characters toward the idea of homeland, due to the radical changes of this space after the revolution. Moaveni writers:

> [Khaleh Farzi] and her husband had moved back to Iran in

1998, after long years in New Jersey. During the first year that my uncle had floated the idea of relocating, she would only say—in a nod to my grandfather's refuge in poetry—'I will only move to places that rhyme with Tehran, such as Milan.' This awkward relationship with reality also characterized her life in Iran, where she spent most of her time reminding us all that 'This is not a country, it is hell' (Moaveni 42).

As reflected in the literature of Iranian women in the diaspora, the subjects try to embody this imagined nation, by creation of a life style resembling their previous life at home. Asayesh refers to this imagined community and the relief the subjects experience when they feel part of it:

> The few smiles are forced, usually in the presence of others, as in the photo of Homajoon [the mother] and a classmate standing in front of the library science building. The only exception was when we joined a gathering of the welcoming crowd of Iranians who lived in Chapel Hill and its environs. They were strange to us because they moved comfortably in a world we found alien; because they seemed unconscious, even when Afsaneh and I stifled giggles, of the English words that littered their Farsi conversation. But they were familiar, too: their eyes and skin and hair, their history, their words. They were a bridge between America and Iran (Asayesh 70).

By clinging to Iranian cultural values, rituals, language and human relations the subjects try to recreate the experience of belonging. Joanne P. Sharp in "Gendering Nationhood: A Feminist Engagement with National Identity" argues this issue:

> The nation is created not through an originary moment or culturally distinct essence but through the repetition of

symbols that come to represent the nation's origin and its uniqueness. National culture and character are ritualistic so that every repetition of its symbols serves to reinforce national identity (Sharp 1996: 98).

Women as transmitters of cultural values have a great role in the formation of the imagined nation and the third space created in between, a homeland abroad. Parisa Milani, in "13 Days" gives us an image of this new "nation" formed based on fantasies in the diaspora, which performs the traditional rituals of the New Year.

> 13 Days after the Iranian New Year
> We gather separately together.
> The sun beats down on
> Bumpy-soft tablecloths as
> Uncles and dads laugh
> At whispered jokes.
> Moms and aunts gossip
> And break pumpkin seeds
> Between their teeth. They
> Speak the tongue with
> Such ease, breaking the seeds
> as though it were something they did
> 'back home'
> (Karim 2006: 332).

Asayesh also writes about the importance of celebrating rituals in the formation and preservation of Iranian cultural identity. The mother, as an Iranian diasporic subject, has not felt the need to do so before the daughter reached the age when she could learn about her roots. But as she grows up, the mother feels responsible for transmitting Iranian cultural values and identity to the daughter and keeps Iranian-ness alive in her and in the next generation(s):

In the past, my celebrations have ranged from nonexistent to token. I have not kept the Iranian calendar since I was a girl of fifteen, living in Chapel Hill and waiting to go home to Iran. But when Mina turned two, I changed my ways. Now we celebrate Charshanbeh-soori 'festive Wednesday' bidding farewell to winter and the old year. We celebrate Norooz ('New Day') when the year changes. We mark Sizdah-bedar, the thirteenth day of the new year, banishing bad fortune in the time-honored way by throwing our *sabzeh*, the greens sprouted especially for Norooz, into flowing water (Asayesh 210).

Celebrating special traditional and religious occasions play an important role in the formation and preservation of their cultural identity. Therefore, the characters try to practice the rituals and provide other characters and the reader with information regarding the details and significance of these collective acts. In "Sabze", Zarreh writes of the tradition of planting seeds for the New Year, as a symbol of fertility and happiness. The greenery will be thrown in a river thirteen days after the New Year eve, hoping for the best to come.

> new seeds
> a familiar plate
> i plant it every year
> and on
> the thirteenth day i throw it
> into a river
> any river will do
> and i hold on to the memory of
> Hope
> until next year
> (Karim 2006: 303).

The narrator performs the ritual only sticking to memories, as she has given up her hope in the outcomes of this symbolic act. She knows now that her days will not be joyous just because she has grown seeds for the New Year. The only functions left for rituals and writing of them is: 1. remembering and imagining an invulnerable cultural identity 2. Belonging to the community of Iranians which needs such traditions to be identified and provide the members with a collective identity. 3. teaching the Iranian traditional rites to the next generation of Iranians or non-Iranian readers, to keep one's own national cultural identity alive.

In "Torches" Susan Atefat-Peckham refers to the ceremony of making fire on the last Tuesday of the year, called *Chaharshanbe Souri*. The Iranian people jump over fires on this night to purify themselves. However, the fire made in the diaspora, as the narrator believes, will not bring luck. The grandfather is dead and his ghost is the only one who keeps the tradition alive through hovering over the fire and seeking for forgiveness, while others are trying to forget who they are. The use of the word "pyres" which is normally used in English in connection with death helps the reader in understanding the implication of the death of the grandfather and the regeneration of the values associated with the ritual in the diaspora.

> This fire is not the flame of luck,
> the pyres they jump over in streets
> at Noruz. These are the lights
> of those who wait, burning 'til embers of forgetting, as they fill
> the tables, while Grandfather hovers in the fluid space
> between flame
> and sky. He is this shining, shimmering
> space, this hot halo, this whispered
> hat held over the house, tipped with
> forgiveness, the fire held close,
> scalding the sky (Karim 2006: 139).

Also the trivial national habits, such as sitting together on a bank (*takht*) in the afternoons and having a chat and a nap are to the narrator of Asayesh's memoir important elements of the Iranian cultural identity and she tries to create the same atmosphere in the diaspora.

> My thirty-sixth birthday is coming up in April. This is to be my present, a *takht* like the ones that sit under the trees in cafes and private homes in Iran, covered with a Persian carpet, the scene of meals and naps and conversations over the samovar.
>
> I have no intention of trying to carry my samovar upstairs, but I harbor visions of starry nights with Neil and me and the children bundled up on a sleeping bag, and lazy afternoons of tea and gossip when my mother and sister visit. Khaleh Farah is even sending me the family *pasheh-band*, the square gauzy tent of mosquito netting that we slept in each summer in Gonabad (Asayesh 203).

Besides rituals, religion is an important part of cutural identity. Some female subjects try to preserve their cultural identity through observing traditional values.

Asayesh in her autobiography elaborates on the issue of cultural identity and religion as follows:

> It is only when I pray that I come close to feeling at peace, allowing myself to believe, little by little, that I can trust the links that bind me to my country, my family, and my past. [...] I say the Arabic words by rote, seeing in my mind's eye my mother and my aunts, my grandmothers and the women who came before them, my own childhood self, all murmuring and bending and rising in a rhythm that spans the centuries (Asayesh 188).

Nevertheless, religious and traditional values of female characters are transformed in the Diaspora. The situation of being migrants from another place and, thereby, of belonging to a minority of "others" often results in a mode of religious change through heightened self-awareness.

> I loved the aspects of my religion that celebrated life. Ramadan, for example, was a time when friends and family, laughing and talking in their black clothes and veils, gathered at sundown to break their fasts with a feast. I was awed and inspired by the concept of fasting and by the faithful way it was carried out all around me. [...] But I hated the gloom and zealotry. My sister and I were endlessly scrutinized and chastised. Did we pray? Our religious relatives wanted to know, clucking in disapproval when we stammered, 'Sometimes'. The veneer of our Western life would crumble at such moments, revealing the religious roots that bound us all (Asayesh 82).

Elsewhere she writes:

> Living in America, with its lofty intellectualism, has robbed me of simple faith, that precious legacy of growing up in a simple land. I realize the essential magic of belief, that its transformative power lies not in *what* you believe but *that* you believe. I begin to see that it is our capacity for awe that links us to the divine (Asayesh 38).

The space of homeland and displacement from it plays a very important role in formation or/and transgression of religious identity of the female subjects of literary works of Iranian Diaspora literature by women. In an interaction between the character's national identity and that of the "Other", cultural and religious values of the characters become dual, always in process and hybrid, as Stuart Hall (Hall 1996) puts it. Therefore, an essentialist definition of Islamic beliefs is no more applicable to the religious behavior of Iranian women in the Diaspora, as a new version of Islam is created among them, which is full of paradoxes and innovations.

For the young generation of diasporic characters who have always lived in the hostland and long to belong, it is not desirable to sacrifice their Westerner "self" for the hybrid and problematic identity of the parents. Aphrodite Désirée Navab, refers to this issue in "Tales left untold":

> How I've tried all my life to be
> No messy ambiguity
> No ambivalent loyalty
> To be
> One
> Whole
> One
> Identity
> The flag of each nation
> In me, stirs little sensation
> No nationalism shouts loud in me
> (Karim 2006: 282).

The distance the Iranian female characters of the second generation, or native-aliens, take from Iranian cultural values is a defense method against marginalization in their new social life. This is more dominant when they are teenagers and young adults trying to know their identity, and sensitive about their social interactions. This is the time of public presence and detachment from families and their values:

> When I was in high school and college, I longed to be delivered of the burdens of the past, to be free to belong in the world of my peers. Now that I lived outside the constraints of family and culture, I discovered in myself a need to belong in ways that transcended the superficial acceptance of my friends (Asayesh 127).

However, the rejection of Iranianness as an integration method gives its place to a strong need to preserve Iranian cultural identity as the subject grows up and overcomes the urge to belong to the new society.

The extreme inferiorization of Iranians in America after the hostage crisis also played an important role in the detachment of Iranian female subjects from national values and their Iranian self. Moaveni writes:

> To be Iranian in the United States during the 1980s meant living perpetually in the shadow of the hostage crisis. Many Iranians dealt with this by becoming the perfect immigrants: successful, assimilated, with flawless, relaxed American English and cheerfully pro-American political sentiments (Moaveni 8).

To avoid prejudice and hostile behavior they washed any sign of Iranian national identity away from their lives. Although these characters may seem fully integrated, they do not fully define themselves as Americans and live an in-between life.

Conclusion

In this chapter, as discussed above, the role of space and displacement in identity formation of female characters of the literary productions of Iranian women in the Diaspora are examined using the post-modern and post-colonial theories of space and gender. Home, City, and homeland change and form the gendered identity and body politics of these subjects. Displacement from home as a space of unification with self and mother, affects the identity and psyche of the subjects. In the second place, living in a Western city which is completely different in density, aesthetic values, and the freedom provided, is a challenging experience for Iranian women in the diaspora and causes sexual, religious and cultural identity crisis. Finally, a shared sense of belonging to a (lost) homeland ties the members of Iranian Diaspora to each other and saves them from loss of identity in the Diaspora. Through memory and imagination, the subjects try to create a sense of belonging and being rooted. However, through their migration subjects become outsiders forever, and a perpetual quest begins to find a way back, and to be "whole" again.

CHAPTER THREE: BILINGUALISM AND GENDER[1]

In the selected poems and memoirs the narrators tell us about the significance of the mother tongue in preserving identity and the role language acquisition plays in integration. Hybridity in terms of language, as a consequence of the in-between identity of the female characters, is another theme of these works. Bilingualism affects the identity formation of the female characters, through their investment in the second language, their social life and their generation. The female characters and the narrators belonging to the first generation of immigrants are expected to stick to the mother tongue and national values and transmit them to the next generation.

The female characters and narrators of the first generation are considered the protectors of the value system of the community of Iranians in the Diaspora. However, this causes a lack of interest in language acquisition. Lack of previous adequate education, which facilitates language acquisition and insufficient contact with the new society and language, are other obstacles that some of the first-generation female characters in these works face. However, the female characters of the second generation eagerly learn English in order to integrate into the new society.

The fight to retain one's own identity via language is an important theme in the works in question. The use of English is significant in some of these works as in parts the writers and female characters adopt a few features of Persian syntax or include Persian words written

---

1   A paper entitled "Bilingualism and Gender in the Literature of Iranian Women in the Diaspora" has been prepared based on the findings in this chapter and published in the *Review of Social Studies (RoSS)* Vol. 2, No.1, 2015.

in the Roman alphabet, which are completely meaningless to an Anglophone reader. This puts the language of the text somewhere between Persian and English, between the language of the characters and that of the host-language readers.

However, for them, English is not just associated with marginality and otherness. It is the language of modern and free countries and it therefore gives the subjects a sense of security when they express their inner conflicts in this language.

Second Language Acquisition and Gender

One of the first requirements of a life in the Diaspora for these female characters is to learn the language of the host country so as to communicate and belong. The process of learning and using this second language affects and is affected by the gendered identities of the characters, their community and the generations to which they belong. Language seems more arbitrary to them in comparison to those who do not experience the Diaspora and bilingualism. As Pavlenko and Lantolf (2000: 169-170) put it:

> The ultimate attainment in second language learning relies on one's agency [...]. While the first language and subjectivities are an indisputable given, the new ones are arrived at by choice... [through] a long, painful, inexhaustive, and, for some, never-ending process of self-translation.

The expectations of the community to which the subject belongs affect her identity and her investments in cultural capital. The reactions of the characters to the expectations of the community in terms of language play a great role in second language use, as Menard-Warwick and Ehrlich have found in their research, admitting the importance of the gendered identity of female characters in language acquisition: "[L]anguage learning is not so much mediated by 'the way that gender identities and gender relations are constructed in (a) community'"

(Ehrlich 1997: 430, in Menard-Warwick 2009: 72), "but rather by the way that individuals *respond* to the gendered expectations that are placed on them by their families and communities" (Menard-Warwick 2009: 72).

The community of Iranian diasporic characters and their families expect the female characters to preserve the mother tongue and the national values instead of passing the boundaries of the community by learning the language, fearing the destruction of the patriarchal structure of traditional families and the community. But to belong to the new society, the subjects need to learn the second language and communicate actively with the new world. Otherwise they will undergo marginalisation and inferiorisation. Responses to the gendered expectations, however, are also constructed and instructed by the power relations in the society and the generation to which the subject belongs. Below I will try to show how the significance of generation and community in the gendered identity and language learning of female characters is reflected in the selected literary and autobiographical texts.

Generations

The motivation of the female characters to learn the new language is related to their investment in a community. As Norton and McKinney (2011: 75) puts it:

> The construct of investment, first introduced by Norton [...], signals the socially and historically constructed relationship of learners to the target language, and their often ambivalent desire to learn and practice it [...]. Norton argued that, if learners invest in a second language, they do so with the understanding that they will acquire a wider range of symbolic and material resources, which will in turn increase the value of their cultural capital.

The investment in the community is different for the first and second generations. The first generation invests in the community of family and Iranians in the diaspora or back in Iran. The community they invest in does not find it necessary or even appropriate for them to speak the language of the new country and blend in. However, the second-generation female characters invest in the community of natives of the host country, as they have more contacts in school or university. This community invites them to learn the language in order to belong.

As Norton and McKinney say, "[A] language learner's motivation is mediated by investments that may conflict with the desire to speak, or, paradoxically, may make it possible for the language learner to claim the right to speak" (Norton & McKinney 2011: 84). The community of Iranians in the Diaspora expects the female characters of the first generation to preserve the mother tongue and teach it to the next generation. This leads to a lack of interest in second language learning. Lack of basic education, which would facilitate language acquisition, and lack of enough social interactions, are other complications that these characters struggle with when learning English. However, the female characters of the second generation learn the second language willingly, as they have more social contacts in the new world and develop integrative motivations. Below, the role of community and the expectation of language learning and its difficulties for the two generations of female characters in the case study will be discussed in greater detail.

a. First Generation

As transmitters and protectors of the value system of the community the female characters of the first generation of immigrants are obliged to stick to the mother tongue and the traditional roles of a woman. The expectations of these communities limit the female characters in their access to new ways of life and language in the host country.

The limitations that the community imposes on the first generation female characters are laid down in the name of preservation of their gendered identity. This causes a lack of interest in language acquisition. In Dumas's work the narrator claims that her mother never learned English well enough to able to read the book she wrote. This was due to the gendered roles of a mother in a traditional Iranian family, not leaving enough time and motivation for her to learn the language of the host country.

> My mother's English prevented her from reading the book. I did, however, let her know what I had written. She gave me her blessing but had a few questions. 'Did you mention that I never left you with a babysitter, even though I could have? Did you mention that I nursed you for over two years and how difficult you were to wean? Did you mention how I was always at home when you returned from school, that you never came home to an empty house?'
> Although none of the above made it into the book, any mother who gives her blessing to a memoir that mocks her accent has the right to tell the world that I was a pain to wean (Dumas 191).

However, investment in the community of Iranians is not the only reason for preserving the mother tongue. Lack of education that facilitates language acquisition is another aspect that is closely related to gender roles and the expectations of the female characters. Dumas writes:

> The problem was that my mother, like most women of her generation, had been only briefly educated. In her era, a girl's sole purpose in life was to find a husband. Having an education ranked far below more desirable attributes such as the ability to serve tea or prepare baklava (Dumas 5).

The mother did not receive an education as a young girl. Her gendered role and function in the community did not require or allow her to acquire the average education the male subjects of her generation and social class could get in the same town in Iran. Therefore, as a middle-aged woman in the Diaspora, having the chance of learning a new language, she lacked the basic knowledge that would facilitate it. If she had learned to look reflexively at language through the study of her own language and basic knowledge of English, offered at Iranian high schools and universities, this might have awaken her curiosity, motivate her to learn this language and facilitate the process of learning.

Another significant barrier for language acquisition in the first generation diasporic characters is lack of sufficient contact with the new society and language in the roles of housewives or employees in family businesses. Norton, in her research on immigrant women, analyses this issue as follows:

> In theorizing the gendered nature of the immigrant language learner's experience, I am concerned not only with the silencing that women experience within the context of larger patriarchal structures in society, but also with the gendered access to the public world that immigrant women, in particular, experience. It is in the public world that language learners have the opportunity to interact with members of the target language community, but it is the public world that is not easily accessible to immigrant women.... [E]ven when such access is granted, the nature of the work available to immigrant women provides few opportunities for social interaction (Norton 2000: 12-13).

Lack of social relations or having limited access to English-speaking society is a major obstacle in learning the second language for the female characters of the first generation. Their traditional role as mother and wife offers them fewer opportunities for social interactions than men or members of the second generation. They are mostly busy with taking care of the family, and their relations are limited to neighbours and hairdressers. In *Funny in Farsi* the characters depend on the husband and father to be the link to the new world. Therefore, there is no need to participate in social life and learn the language and culture.

> Moving to America was both exciting and frightening, but we found great comfort in knowing that my father spoke English. Having spent years regaling us with stories about his graduate years in America, he had left us with the distinct impression that America was his second home. My mother and I planned to stick close to him, letting him guide us through the exotic American landscape that he knew so well. We counted on him not only to translate the language but also to translate the culture, to be a link to this most foreign of lands (Dumas 8).

However, the English that the father speaks is limited to academic terms and usages. Throughout the work, the daughter declares her independence from the father by learning English when she goes to school, and she becomes more involved with the native community. Yet, this was not possible for the father as an engineer using English only in his workplace. The mother was never able to learn the language properly and spoke English with mistakes, which led to misunderstandings and inferiorisation. She also had to use her daughter as a translator or limit her relations to the community of Farsi speakers. The narrator writes, "I no longer encourage my parents to learn English. I've given up" (Dumas 12). In *Iranian and Diasporic Literature in the 21st Century* Grassian explains: "While she never directly states it, it is possible that Dumas has come to this resigned position because of the difficulties that she and her parents have faced while trying to assimilate" (Grassian 2013: 130).

As mentioned above, the female characters of the first generation in the memoirs and literary works under discussion have an instrumental investment in second language acquisition. The community they associate themselves with is the community of Iranians in the Diaspora with the patriarchal structure expecting them to preserve and transmit national identity and mother tongue, fearing the "possible selves" (Pavlenko & Norton 2007: 670) that the female subject may become in the new cultural and linguistic space. Lack of basic education and social contact are other reasons for problems in second language learning in the first generation diasporic characters.

b. Second Generation

Unlike the female characters of the first generation, those of the second generation are generally eager to learn the language and culture of the host country. Firstly, because they are in permanent contact with the English speaking world in the schools and daily life, they have more chance to learn the language. Secondly, the need to belong in the new world is greater in the second generation, as they are more involved in social life, and the key to this integration is the English language. They try to form identities in the Diaspora that are different from those of the first generation. These new identities require changes in the attitude towards language. As Eckert and McConnell-Ginet declare, these changes are the results of the social conditions:

> The linguistic changes are not something that have [sic] simply washed over the younger generation; they are the result of girls' finding ways of constructing kinds of selves that were not available to earlier generations. They are the result of social and linguistic strategies (Eckert & McConnell-Ginet 2004: 329).

While the first generation of female characters has an "instrumental" motivation for learning English in the Diaspora, the motivation of female characters of the second generation is "integrative". Norton and McKinney use the definitions of these terms given by Gardner & Lambert (1972):

> [I]nstrumental motivation references the desire of language learners to learn an L2 for utilitarian purposes, such as employment, while integrative motivation references the desire

to learn a language to successfully integrate with the target language community (Norton & McKinney 2011: 74).

The integrative motivation of diasporic female characters of the second generation is due to the need to belong in the new world. They do not want to live a life in-between as their parents do, and would like to experience equality in English-speaking society. The power relations included in the knowledge of the second language persuade the characters to learn the second language and consider the mother tongue as a burden. Zjaleh Hajibashi in her poem "Where Does My Language Lie?" describes this condition metaphorically:

> [...]
> where I lie with which language
> unspeakable
> duplicity
> took me
> draws me
>
> twice
> subdued
>
> deep into my other tongue's mouth another tongue
> mine
>
> to
>   mute
> not saying
> this
> not
> saying
> (Karim 2006: 43)

The speaker may feel guilty for inferiorising her mother tongue, but she finds no other way to fight the marginalisation imposed on her from society. The duplicity the character faces in her identity is manifested in the two languages, the two tongues, and she finds no other way than to mute the mother tongue. Asayesh, in her memoir, also refers to this issue when the female character feels inferiorised and marginalised in the society and wants to defend her status by speaking unaccented English and rejecting her Iranian self.

> See, I am fluent in English! I have no accent! I'm like you. Don't consign me to the trash heap, where the unforgivably different belong. Don't look at me as if I were an animal at the zoo, an object of curiosity and spurious compassion.
> This inner dialogue fills me with shame, yet I am helpless against it. I have become a party to my own disenfranchisement. The worst part of being told in a thousand ways, subtle and not, that one is inferior is the way that message worms itself into the heart. It is not enough to battle the prejudice of others, one must also battle the infection within (Asayesh 210-11).

To the character "Gelareh" in this work, belonging in the new world means rejection of the language and membership of the community of Iranians. She does not find herself alone in this. Throughout the narrative, she meets other female characters of the second generation who avoid using the mother tongue and reject their Iranian identity. Asayesh continues:

> The need to belong is a powerful thing. It pits those of us who are children of other worlds against ourselves and one another.
> It made the Iranian clerk I encountered a few years ago at Bloomingdale's, in Rockville, Maryland, stare coldly when I spoke to her in Farsi. She rang up my sale without a word.
> A few months later, when an Iranian handed me the num-

> bered tag I took into the dressing room of another depart-
> ment store, I was careful to thank her in English. I preten-
> ded that I did not recognize the almond skin, arched eye-
> brows, and glossy hair of a countrywoman (Asayesh 210).

This sense of powerlessness and inferiority causes resistance to learn-ing the mother tongue and Iranian culture. These struggles and resist-ances to defend the subject against the sense of being different in terms of language and, by extension, identity, are strongest when the subjects are in the community of school and college. They need to be accepted and belong. They try to avoid in-betweenness by sticking to the dominant language and culture and ignoring the expectation of the family or community of Iranians to learn the mother tongue and na-tional values. However, this does not mean that the mother tongue and culture can be completely ignored. Menard-Warwick, using the ideas of Davies and Harré (1990: 48) and Weeden (1987), explains that des-pite social conditions, the characters are able to make decisions regard-ing their participation in a discourse.

> Like Weeden, they [Davies and Harré] explore how dis-
> courses define the people who use them in terms of subject
> positions, that is, socially recognisable categories. However,
> they also emphasise that human beings can make choices
> in regards to their discursive participation, choices that of-
> ten stem from an individual's 'history as a subjective being,
> that is, the history of one who has been in multiple posi-
> tions and engaged in different forms of discourses'
> (Menard-Warwick 2009: 38).

Some of the female characters of the second generation establish a need and choose to belong to the Iranian national identity and mother tongue as adults, because they have overcome the feeling of inferiority that is associated with them. The speaker in Parissa Milani's poem "American Again" knows that the key to belonging is the language and that she cannot be considered Iranian if she speaks English or Farsi with an English accent. Therefore, she chooses silence so that the community of Iranians to accept her. However, she knows that it would be impossible for her not to return to the American language and culture which she knows best. She wonders if it is possible for her to return to her American self and language whenever she wishes, without being expelled by the community of Iranians.

> I am Iranian
> until I open my mouth. Then
> I am American.
>
> But if I promise to not even breathe
> through my mouth, will you take me in?
> Will you take me to the Caspian Sea
> and tell me it's always been so close?
> [...]
> Will you understand when
> it gets hard for me to
> breathe easy and I become
> American again?
> (Karim 2006: 220)

Although the idea of not even breathing through the mouth, out of which come the words with American accent, to avoid any sign of Americanness seems exaggerating, but it shows how important it is for her to present herself as a Persian native speaker to the community of Iranians and belong to this community.

This double identity and belonging to two different languages and worlds lead to in-betweenness and, paradoxically, belonging to neither language and culture. In her poem "Tales Left Untold", Aphrodite Desiree Navab describes this situation using the metonymy of "tongue" for language:

My tongue is twisted
My tongue is tied
My tongue is torn with all the lies
Each time I turn it this way and that
An unfamiliar sound spins its way out
One half screams for the other to come
The other half stands there completely numb
One half knows not what the other half speaks
One half scorns what the other half seeks
My tongue, it trips me
Leading me there
Trapping me in the storyteller's snare
One half leaves while the other half stays
One half sees what the other betrays (Karim 2006: 287)

The character's identity is torn in two, and each half has its own language. The two selves and tongues, however, are in need of each other, although they are never at peace. This oscillation between two languages and identities can lead to a constant fear of losing one half while sticking to the other. The characters are scared of the people they may become, the "possible selves". As Pavlenko and Norton say, citing Wegner and Markus & Nurius:

[Possible selves] represent individuals' ideas of what they might become, what they would like to become, and what they are afraid of becoming, thus linking cognition, behavior, and motivation. For both Wegner and Markus and Nurius, possible selves, linked to membership in imagined communities, shape individuals' present and future decisions and behaviors and provide an evaluative and interpretive context for such decisions, behaviors, and their outcomes (Pavlenko & Norton 2007: 670).

The character Gelareh in Asayesh's memoir tries to reduce her fear of the possible selves she or her children may become by insisting on transmitting the Iranian cultural identity to the next generation (mostly the daughter as her continuation) through teaching the mother tongue. Asayesh writes:

> I know that language is the lifeblood of culture. Language is the self, reflected and clothed in nouns and verbs and adjectives. Without Farsi, the Iranian in Mina will shrivel up and die. Even as I think this, I know that my greatest fear is of my own inner shriveling, not Mina's. In guarding Mina's heritage, I guard my own, for they are linked. My daughter, this piping voice in my house speaking the words I learned at my mother's knee, is a lifeline to my first self [...]. I feel like a beached whale, slowly drying up (Asayesh 213).

The cultural identity of the subject is here deeply associated with the mother tongue. As Elahi writes in "Translating the Self: Language and Identity in Iranian-American Women's Memoirs":

> These images (a beached whale, the inner self shriveling up and dying, the self as the victim of erosion) represent a relatively static sense of identity but a dynamic sense of language. They naturalise the self as inert, and lead Asayesh to fall back onto fairly rigid distinctions between Iran and America (Elahi 2006: 470).

The narrator in Asayesh's memoir does not believe in hybrid identity and draws a clear line between Iranian and American identities. This is also the case when it comes to languages. Although she refers to language as fluid, this does not mean that her two languages can dissolve each other. "Language, I remind myself, is fluid. What is lost can be regained. This time next year, when we go back to Iran, it will be the English words that take a back seat. Bilingualism, like biculturalism, is a seesaw" (Asayesh 213). The oscillation that the character experiences in terms of identity is extended to the languages she speaks. As Elahi puts it:

> For Asayesh, language is (or languages are) both seesaw and sea; their access to truth and the richness of their textures can only be experienced in an alternation between one and another tongue, not in the space between or on one side alone (Elahi 2006: 470).

The character seeks to belong to both Iranian and American identities, but not a third hybrid one. The dominance of the Iranian self requires the repression of the American one. Asayesh describes this condition in this way:

> Sometimes I wake up in the middle of the night, the words of my first language bursting into my mouth from some long-suppressed place. For days afterward, the English words feel like foreign objects on my tongue, metallic and cold, like the loose filling of a tooth. I walk around full of hidden despair until I manage once again to forget my childhood self (Asayesh 174).

To make a compromise and a relationship between these two languages, and consequently between the two selves, the main character in Moaveni's *Lipstick Jihad* tries to translate from Persian to English. Translating provides the character with a chance to make a bridge between the two languages and therefore the two identities that are always in conflict with each other and leave the character in a permanent detachment, and, as she puts it, a "sense of foreignness."

> The urge to translate, this preoccupation with language I had dragged around with me, had been a resistance to the sense of foreignness I felt everywhere—a distraction from the restlessness that followed me into each hemisphere. If I could only have conquered words, purged from my Farsi

any trace of accent, imported the imagery of Persian verse into English prose, I had thought, then the feeling of displacement would go away (Moaveni 234).

The female characters of the second generation of Iranians in the Diaspora, as reflected in the case study, live with a paradox and conflict between two selves and two languages, which is a result of bilingualism and biculturalism in the Diaspora. No matter how hard they try to preserve their linguistic selfhood, hybridity in language and identities is inevitable as an important consequence of the Diaspora. Below I will explain the characteristics of linguistic hybridity in the texts mentioned.

Writing in the Language of the Other

The stylistic characteristics of the selected literary and autobiographical works are quite significant. The authors have chosen to write in English as it is the language they have mastered as a written language in the American education system. Besides, writing in English can make their works accessible to a larger audience and their voices can be heard more widely. This means that they are writing for the Other, using the language of the Other. But one of the most important reasons is the freedom they feel to write everything in English. However, this does not satisfy them, as they also want to make a connection with the members of the community of Iranians in the diaspora. This will give them a sense of belonging and attachment. To overcome this paradox, they develop a hybrid language.

> Organic, unconscious hybridity is a feature of the historical evolution of all languages. Applying it to culture and society more generally, we may say that despite the illusion of boundedness, cultures evolve historically through unreflective borrowings, mimetic appropriations, exchanges and inventions. [...] Intentional hybrids create an ironic double

consciousness, a collision between differing points of views on the world (Bakhtin 1981: 360).

Hybridity, as Bakhtin says, is the fate of a language. The "double consciousness" of the subjects in the Iranian Diaspora makes them create a hybrid language that is capable of transmitting their inner conflicts. They write in a threshold language, a variety of English that is enriched with Persian words and grammar and is understandable to the members of the community. It is a language that belongs to this community. On the other hand, it gives them the advantages of writing in English as a dominant language and the language of freedom. Elahi, using the term "accented identity" introduced by Taghi Modarressi in *Writing with an Accent* (1992) writes "The notion of accented identity, and specifically of accented writing, can help us understand how Iranian-Americans might transform the trauma of a language lost into the celebration of a self regained or reconstructed, a translation of identity into a new language or through a dialectical relationship between two languages" (Elahi 2006: 464). Below is a discussion of the dimensions of this accented language that the female characters of the selected literary works use, with their hyphenated and in-between identities.

a. Creation of Personal English

The implied authors in the works mentioned have a specific usage of English, which includes Persian words or proverbs roughly translated into English. This enables them to write for the community they belong to, or would like to belong to—the community of Iranians in the diaspora. As Eckert & McConnell-Ginet say in *Language and Gender*, each community has its own language use.

> [P]atterns of language choice are built into the social fabric of the community. Speakers may borrow lexical items from one language to another, they may use different language in different situations and with different people, they may use more than one language in the same conversation—

code-switching from one turn to another, or within sentences. These strategies make social meaning in much the same way as variation within the same language (Eckert & McConnell-Ginet 2003: 270).

Use of this language form gives a sense of separateness from the English-speaking American natives. This leads to the formation of a unique social identity based on the insider/outsider boundaries. Bahrampour writes, "It is fun to speak like this, to lazily pick the best words from each side and form a fused language you'd have to be one of us to understand" (Bahrampour 191).

Some instances of this fused language in the texts occur when the subject brings in Persian words with or without an introduction. This accented language is organic to the accented identity of the characters, as Modaressi suggests (1992: 7-9). Another very good example is that of Bahrampour:

> My Farsi life swims darkly below my English life [...] The more I speak it, the more I notice I've picked up words I don't remember having learned. In fact, there are some words I only know in Farsi, words my family uses no matter which language we are speaking. *Khash-khash* is a hard green oblong pod the size of my fist, which Ali and I split open to shake out handfuls of white seeds that pop between our teeth like tiny pearls. *Toot* is a musky purple or white berry that grows on trees, and *joob* is the trench between street and sidewalk that carries water through the city, getting slower and blacker the further south it goes (Bahrampour 50).

Discussing this excerpt from Bahrampour's memoir, Elahi writes:

> The implied authors resist translation as they believe this will blur the connotations of the word and its vocal characteristics. In contrast to Asayesh's beached whale, Bahram-

pour's Persian is almost like a shark (swimming darkly) below the surface of conscious speech (Elahi 2006: 471).

Through the language, the implied author tries to draw a line between those who belong to the community and can understand the language and those who are outsiders.

Moaveni writes: "I realized that some of my most integral parts resisted translation. It was only in not being able to transport them into another language that I saw how much they mattered" (Moaveni 68). This inability to translate or avoidance of translation differentiate the language of the diasporic subject from that of the Other, and reminds her how important these words are as metonymies for her Iranian self.

Even when the subject translates a Persian dialogue in English, she does not try to create a perfectly understandable text for the Other. On the contrary, the translations keep the grammatical format of the mother tongue, the proverbs are translated word for word and no equivalent is given as in Bahrampour's text:

> To keep my head warm... [to keep someone busy]
> Don't be tired [Keep up the good work]
> God take care of you [God bless you]
> (Bahrampour 141, my translation).

The subjects try to enrich the English language by using Persian words that do not have an English equivalent. The main character "Firoozeh", in *Funny in Farsi,* uses Persian words for familial relations as they are more exact than the ones in English. And she continues using them throughout the memoir as normal words.

> Growing up in Iran, I was surrounded not by snow or tann
> ed people, but by relatives. Not surprisingly, my native lan-
> guage, Persian, contains many more precise words for relat-
> ives than does the English language. My father's brothers
> are my *amoo.* My mother's brother is a *dye-yee.* My aunts'
> husbands are either *shohar ammeh or shohar khaleh,* de-

pending on which side of the family they are from. In English, all these men are simply my 'uncles.' Only one word describes their children in English, 'cousin,' whereas in Persian, we have eight words to describe the exact relationship of each cousin (Dumas 96-97).

Farsi is used as a means of resistance against the Other language, English, in some of the works of the case study. The characters use English in a significant way: they use Persian grammar in translating a Persian dialogue, or Persian words in English alphabets. This puts language somewhere between Persian and English. This language is specific for the member of the community of Iranians in the diaspora, the community that the characters long to belong to. Through this language the subjects can manifest their dual identities properly.

However, for some of the female subjects of the selected literary works of Iranian women in the Diaspora, English is not only associated with inferiorisation and marginality. Their fluency in English and the freedom connected with this language encourages them to write in English. Below I will elaborate on this in more detail.

b. Using English as the Language of Taboos and Secrets

English for the implied authors of the mentioned works seems to be the language in which they can write easily, as they are all educated in western systems. They admit that, using English, they can talk about forbidden aspects of Iranian culture. The reason may be the close association of culture and language: the taboos in a culture are not to be performed by the members of the community and not to be spoken about in its language.

English has become an important part of the identity of the female subjects of, specifically, the second generation. It is through this language that they can express the inner conflicts between their two selves. Their knowledge of Farsi is not sufficient to fulfil all their linguistic needs as they have learned it only in a domestic environment.

One of the female characters in Moaveni's work names it "kitchen Farsi," a colloquial Persian limited to "Gossiping with family and whining to my parents," with "no special fluency," leaving the speakers "ill-equipped to hold abstract conversations with the highly literate" (Moaveni 89). The narrator of Moaveni's memoir, with the same knowledge of Farsi, mentions that she uses English words in her Farsi conversations and makes a hybrid language to be able to communicate. But trying to speak pure Farsi she realizes "that without English, I, as I knew myself, ceased to exist" (Moaveni 89). As Elahi puts it "Moaveni tells us explicitly of the pain and violence she feels in losing a self that exists neither in the United States nor in Iran, but in the English language" (Elahi 2006: 472). English has become a part of the identity of the subject as much as Farsi, the mother tongue.

Another important reason for the sense of freedom in writing in English is the association of this language as the language of "the Land of the Free", with security and liberty. The narratives associated with the mother tongue are mostly devastating while English reminds the subject of successful challenges to win freedom. Moaveni explains it in her work as follows:

> [T]he very act of speaking English invoked a sense of freedom. It was the language in which I had fought many battles, but it was also the language of an alternative existence in which I never felt fear. It was unpolluted by the brutality of the things I heard and spoke about in Farsi, like arrests of activists and the killings of dissidents. Of course I wrote about them in English, but exported across the border of another language, their horror was somehow muted (Moaveni 89).

Fear, no matter how imaginary, is dominant in the mentality of the subject when she speaks in Farsi, while English reminds her of security. Therefore, she prefers to speak of her private life and social criticism in English to feel more at peace. However, even in private life and issues such as love and sexuality, Farsi does not help the character express herself. Moaveni writes:

> I tried to explain, dismayed to see notions like 'I need space' evaporate into meaninglessness in Farsi. It was as though the soft, soap-opera lighting of English had been switched off, and replaced by the harsh, fluorescent glare of Farsi (Moaveni 68).

As the notions of love and lust are differently understood in the Iranian and American cultures, the vocabulary and expressions for them are untranslatable in the language of the other culture. Also the taboo words that are unspeakable in Farsi can be mentioned in English. These includes sexual talks, in Moaveni's memoir, or the use of swear words in Asayesh's work. Gelareh, the narrator of the latter memoir writes: "I use too many swear words in English but know none in Farsi" (Asayesh 173). Swear words and sexual talks are taboos for female characters in Iranian culture. The characters learn such expression only when they are in contact with the colloquial and underground language, although they would not use them freely. The second generation female characters who learn the mother tongue in the families and have not had access to the underground language spoken in Iran do not know the Farsi vocabulary for them. But due to their permanent access to the colloquial English in the host land they learn the English swear words easily. Besides, in the Western culture in which they are brought up referring to these subjects is not gendered, and the characters can use these expressions openly. The implied authors and the female characters of the selected texts feel free to swear and talk about sex in English as their American selves, informed by the English language, allow them to do so, while their Iranian selves prohibit it.

The incapacity of family members to understand colloquial English gives the subjects a chance to use this language for their secret talks and writing. Gelareh in Asayesh's memoir says: "By the time we returned to Tehran, English was the language in which my sister and I communicated best. It was the language of our private exchanges, our furious fights and games and bargains" (Asayesh 66-67). Speaking in English, the subject can benefit from the freedom achieved through her unique knowledge of vernacular English. The family members in Iran speak English very little or not at all. Therefore, they cannot observe and control the secret conversations of the two girls. So they can enjoy their freedom although they are living in a rather oppressive atmosphere for female characters.

As we have seen above, the implied authors and characters have a dual relationship with the English language. It detaches them from the community of Iranians in the Diaspora and Iran, but at the same time it is the language that gives them freedom to write about this community and speak of different aspects of their identity without fear. It is the language of modern and free countries and, therefore, it gives them a sense of security when they express their inner conflicts in this language.

Conclusion

Second language acquisition affects the identity formation of female characters of the recent literary works of Iranian female writers in the Diaspora. The generations to which the female immigrants belong are of great importance in language acquisition and use. As transmitters and protectors of the value system of the community, the female characters of the first generation of immigrants are supposed to preserve the mother tongue. On the contrary, the female characters of the second generation are usually eager to learn the language and culture of the host country as an integration requirement.

The freedom the subjects feel when writing in English, enables them to use this language to express their inner feelings and identity concerns. However, they are also willing to use their mother tongue as the best means to represent their Iranian identity. As they are always in-between two cultures, they experience an aporia in their language choice. As Elahi argues, speaking of some of the works mentioned in this research, "[T]hese narratives of self do speak in a language between; they are written with an accent, or, at the very least they narrate the process of losing that accent" (Elahi 2006: 479). This in-betweenness leads to the creation of a personal hybrid (English) language and finds a home in English by mixing it with Persian words and proverbs. This is the language they can belong to and express themselves with, the language of the third space they live in, the space in between, the threshold.

CHAPTER FOUR: WRITING AND GENDER

There is a significant body of autobiographical works of Iranian female writers in the Diaspora. The early works are mostly social and political, as writing about private life has been a taboo for Iranian women. In the last decade more autobiographical works have emerged which focus on the more private aspect of the lives of characters in the Diaspora and their identity crises. However, little critical work has so far been done on these recent autobiographical works. In this chapter the autobiographical writing (memoir, poetry and short story) of the second generation of Iranian female writers will be introduced and analyzed using post-colonial and post-modern theories of autobiography and gender.

Firstly, a general survey of the autobiographies of Iranian women in Iran and in the Diaspora and their difference in form and content will be given here. Then the significance of writing for the female characters in the selected works will be analyzed. It is through writing that they can confess and recover from the traumas they have experienced. Shame narratives, quest for the "self" and maternal stories are also included in some of these autobiographical texts. Besides, they express their own social and political theories in their autobiographical writings.

Iranian Women and Writing

Throughout history, Iranian women have not been as active as men in the field of literature, due to their lack of required education, social interactions, and financial support. Besides, the Iranian feminine tradition of "Silence" has always prevented women from writing and bringing their private life into the public realm. According to Najmabadi in

Women's Autobiographies in Contemporary Iran, the most suitable genre for the first writings of women was poetry because of its ambiguity (Najmabadi 5-6).

Hanaway in "Half-voices: Persian Women's Lives and Letters" believes that autobiography writing in Iran was not common because of the separation of private from public life (Hanaway 1990: 55). Autobiographies of Iranian women in the past have mostly focused on social questions, and have certain common characteristics; they have a sense of self that is deeply rooted in the public domain, tend to destroy a false image the readers might have from Iran, and include a firm belief of the narrator in knowing her "self" and her society. The memoir of the activist and academician Azar Nafisi entitled *Reading Lolita in Tehran: A Memoir in Books* (2003) is a good example of such autobiographical writings.

In these works the subject defines herself in relation to the men in her life as she depends on them and does not have enough experience to establish her own theories of social life. Among these works one can name the political autobiography of the Queen of Iran, Farah Pahlavi, entitled *An Enduring Love: My Life with the Shah: A Memoir* (2005).

Milani in "Veiled Voices: Women's Autobiographies in Iran" claims that the paradox of women's emancipation and ideal femininity are presented in the early autobiographies of Iranian women in the diaspora (Milani 1990: 14). Besides, she argues that the genre of autobiography has been used as a resistance against the undermining of individualism in Iranian culture, through proving the writer a tribune to express her own ideas (Milani 1990: 12).

However, the Iranian female writers of the second generation develop a need for expressing themselves and feel free to do so, as their gendered identity and roles have gone through a change. Besides, using another language and another cultural space provides them with the freedom to write about anything tabooed in the Iranian culture. Finally, the popularity of the memoir in the U.S., where large numbers of

Iranians live, opened up the literary sphere rapidly to new voices and gave the Iranian female authors a chance to tell their stories (Atlas 25).

Discussing the similarities and differences of the autobiographical works of the first and second generation Iranian female writers in the U.S. Motlagh in "Towards a Theory of Iranian American Life Writing: Iranian American Literature" writes:

> While first-generation authors are still invested in the depiction of a national story and the possibility of a return to power in the home country, members of the second generation are motivated by different goals [...]. Current memoirists sense the fragmentary nature of the world they live in and simply want to claim that fragmentariness as their own condition. The recent memoirs are no longer intended exclusively to educate Americans about Iran; they are equally invested in teaching themselves and one another about diaspora, a word newly adopted by Iranian Americans to describe their condition (Motlagh 2008: 29).

Malek in "Memoir as Iranian Exile Cultural Production: A Case Study of Marjane Satrapi's Persepolis Series" refers to these memoirs as "unique forms of exil[ic] cultural production", and regards their publication and popularity a positive step towards the vision of Iranian Americans who consider themselves to be "in exile", but at the same time aim for the recognition of their identity in the US social and cultural system (Malek 354).

The autobiographical works of the second generation of female writers in the diaspora are not limited to memoirs or short prose texts and include poetry, especially in the first person. The recent autobiographical prose and poetry by Iranian female writers in the diaspora tends to refer to the identity issues of the characters, as well as the social and political situation in Iran and in the diaspora. Below, the function of autobiographical writing for these authors, and the characteristics of their works will be discussed.

Autobiographical Works of the Second Generation of Iranian Female Writers in the Diaspora

The concept of memoir writing has not been a part of literary tradition in Iranian culture. However, in the diaspora some of the Iranian writers use this genre with some deviations from the typical characteristics. The narrator in the "Magical Chair of Nails: Becoming a Writer in a Second Language" by Roya Hakakian seems to find the Western idea of writing different from the Iranian tradition. She writes:

> I come from a culture in which writing is a metaphysical act. In Persian, a poet doesn't write poetry, she 'tells' it. That subtle shift from writing to telling had long defined my expectations of how writing should feel. Telling seems as natural and effortless as casual speech. Picking up a pen —or typing as I do—becomes the same as opening one's mouth and humming a tune.
> Telling has no trace of sweating. To do the kind of writing that I needed to do, I had to first unlearn most of my Iranian education. Writing is not telling. I stopped looking for inspiration to come from some superhuman heaven. The seat of writing is in the human mind. Its manifestation expresses not only the passion of that mind but also its fashion-how a mind sees and deciphers the world and how it presents that learning with clarity and simplicity (Karim 2006: 258).

Writers in the Diaspora need to change their understanding of writing if they want to produce autobiographical works in a western culture. However, this does not mean that their works follow the features associated with this genre completely. Laurie Stone in *Close to the Bone: Memoirs of Hurt, Rage, and Desire* suggests that in the U.S. a clear pattern had emerged by 1997; memoirs are classified under one of two categories: victim stories or shame narratives (Stone 1997:37). It will be argued here that this classification applies to the contemporary autobiographical writings (prose and poetry) of second generation of Iranian female writers in the Diaspora. Besides, I suggest three other main themes for these autobiographical works: quest for identity, narratives about mother figures, and expressing personal social and political theories. The authors under discussion mostly combine these themes and their works do not fall into one category only.

Besides the autobiographical works in prose, here I will analyze the autobiographical poetry of the selected second generation Iranian female diasporic authors. Brendan Galvin in his essay "The Contemporary Poet and the Natural World" claims that the recent first person poetry is a form of confession (Galvin 130). However, as Graham and Sontag in *After Confession: Poetry as Autobiography* argue, the confessional poetry can embody universal and social matters. They write: "first-person lyrics can embrace a larger social vision, achieving revelation over narcissism, universal resonance over self-referential anecdote" (Graham & Sontag 2001: 6). They suggest that first-person poetry is more than a narcissistic representation of personal feelings and can refer to universal meanings.

The main themes of the autobiographical poetry and prose are mostly similar in the selected autobiographical works but with its highly metaphorical, symbolic and concise language, poetry in the first person can be regarded as an intensified autobiography.

a. Victim Stories

Motlagh claims that in the contemporary memoirs of second generation of Iranian-American female writers the narrators "typically portray themselves as victims both of the Iranian Revolution of 1979 and the invisibility of their community in the American schema of multiculturalism" (Motlagh 2008: 28-29).

As Miriam Fuchs in *The Text is Myself: Women's Life Writing and Catastrophe* claims, "in autobiographies writers seek safe ground and ultimately survival and reconciliation as well as a means of resistance or protest [...] Autobiography may be a pretext for trying to reconstruct what the catastrophe has damaged". She continues that "it is the catastrophe that causes their gender, race, location, and political and personal histories to intersect in imagined, imaginative, or patently strategic life strategies" (Fuchs 2004: 4).

One of the traumatic experiences reflected in some of the works is life in American cities after the hostage taking crisis. Dumas writes of the radical change in the behavior of the previously friendly neighbors during this time: They write anti-Iranian slogans and their children chase the narrator, shouting I-ran ... I-ran. Her mother suggests denying the Iranian nationality in public, fearing of the harassments of the Americans. This has been a traumatic experience for the character.

> During our stay in Newport Beach, the Iranian Revolution took place and a group of Americans were taken hostage in the American embassy in Tehran. Overnight, Iranians living in America became, to say the least, very unpopular. For some reason, many Americans began to think that all Iranians, despite outward appearances to the contrary, could at any given moment get angry and take prisoners. People always asked us what we thought of the hostage situation. 'It's awful', we always said.
> This reply was generally met with surprise. We were asked our opinion on the hostages so often that I started reminding people that they weren't in our garage. My mother solved the problem by claiming to be from Russia or 'Torekey'. (Dumas 39)

To avoid discriminations the main character decides to change her Iranian name into an easy American one; Julie. However, not only she did not feel belonged, but also "fake".

> Thus I started sixth grade with my new, easy name and life became infinitely simpler. People actually remembered my

name, which was an entirely refreshing new sensation. All was well until the Iranian Revolution, when I found myself with a new set of problems. Because I spoke English without an accent and was known as Julie, people assumed I was American. This meant that I was often privy to their real feelings about those 'damn I-raynians'. It was like having those X-ray glasses that let you see people naked, except that what I was seeing was far uglier than people's underwear. It dawned on me that these people would have probably never invited me to their house had they known me as Firoozeh. I felt like a fake (Dumas 65).

Dumas in *Funny in Farsi* uses irony while writing of the difficulties the main character and her family have gone through in the Diaspora. The process of assimilation the character and her family have gone through as immigrants is mostly narrated with humor, which makes it difficult to define as traumatic experience. Also Grassian in *Iranian and Diasporic Literature in the 21st Century: A Critical Study* refers to the denial of the problems of integration in the Diaspora by Dumas in her work.

For Dumas, the process of assimilating does not seem especially emotionally taxing for immigrants, nor does Dumas suggest that she and her family have at all been belittled by their attempt to acculturate. Rather, to Dumas, the American Dream is less of a dream and more of a reality for immigrants (Grassian 2013: 147).

Garassian continues by bringing an example from the text referring to the pains she and her parents have gone through:

If there is any evidence that Dumas believes that the process of assimilation for diasporic Iranians (or immigrants in general) is challenging, it is when she tells us, 'I no longer encourage my parents to learn English. I've given up' (12). While she never directly states it, it is possible that Dumas has come to this resigned position because of the difficulties that she and her parents have faced while trying to assimilate. If so, this is a portion of Dumas's memoir that she does not really focus upon in *Funny in Farsi* (Grassian 2013: 147).

As mentioned above, Dumas mentions the pains of assimilation she and her family went through in her memoir and I would disagree with Grassian that the only reference to the trauma of integration is when the narrator gives up asking her parents to learn English. However, I agree with Grassian's claim regarding the underestimation of the traumas of immigration in Dumas's work. It seems that through irony she wants to fight the inferiorization which life in the diaspora has caused. As Donna Haraway (1991) declares, "[i]rony is about humor and serious play", destabilizing relations of power through a tactical use of rhetoric.

Some of the Iranian-American female authors have referred to the issues of victimization also in their autobiographical poetry. Persis Karim in "Baba's Passing—February 2005" portrays her father as a victim of the Iranians' bad wishes for Americans after the revolution. She writes:

In the snow-covered streets,
alleys of Tehran, people
hail taxis they cannot see.
It is the largest snowfall since 1971,
the twenty-sixth anniversary of the revolution.
Red and green lights strung up
celebrate, not Christmas,
but the holiday for those gathered
in heavy coats, shouting, '*Marg bar Amrika*'
'Death to America!'
Here in America, death
has arrived at my house. My father, who left that place

> more than fifty years ago has faded into
> the white light of winter.
> The week-long vigil
> at his bedside, waiting
> for a sign is over.
> (Karim 2006: 129)

Some of the literary works of the contemporary female writers in the Diaspora who are not living in the U.S. are also confession narratives as the subjects experience the same traumas of revolution, war, leaving their homes, marginalization as women and/or immigrants in the host society. In "The Sun Is a Dying Star" Niloofar Kalaam, an Iranian-Canadian, tells the story of "Laila", an Iranian activist who has experienced the trauma of imprisonment in Iran.

> Once, only once I thought I might die, I say. 'It was midday and they called me. They called my name. They asked me to fetch my *chador* and come. They always called those who were to be executed at midday. My sentence was not death, but it happened sometimes. I was sure the time had come.' The strangest thing was that I did not feel anything. No fear, no sorrow, nothing. The only thing I thought as I was being escorted down the hallway was that I had wanted to do many things... (Karim 2006: 22).

Also Negin Neghabat in "Raw Walnuts" refers to the marginalization she feels in her daily life in the diapora. She writes: "People's smiles and compliments there, in my first country, stood in such massive contrast to the cold, harsh treatment I received in the country that eventually became my second home—Germany" (Karim 2006: 133).

In "Soleiman's Silence" Yalfani tells the story of an immigrant living in Toronto who never spoke, although he was not dumb and knew English. Everyone in the community has his own idea why he does not speak, which includes projection of self-experienced traumas:

Some believed Soleiman was bored by living in exile, that he was homesick. These people had a strong reason for their own silence, not for Soleiman's. They said exile pushes people into isolation, seclusion and finally silence (Karim 297).

As we have seen above, victim stories are recurrent in the literary autobiographical writings of the second generation Iranian female writers in the Diaspora. The traumas of revolution, war, migration and assimilation to the new society, and their influence on the psyche and behavior of the characters are mentioned in these works. Confessing these pains can help the characters overcome their obsession with the past.

b. Narratives of Shame/Guilt

Narrations of shame and guilt are frequently included in these works. Below, the reasons for shame and guilt feelings of the selected authors and the significance of confessing them through writing will be discussed.

Firstly I would like to define the concepts of shame and guilt and underline the similarities and differences between these feelings. Here I use the ideas of Wong & Tsai in their interesting chapter "Cultural models of shame and guilt" in the *Handbook of Self-Conscious Emotions:*

> Whereas shame occurs when one is negatively evaluated by others for behaving inappropriately, involves global and stable attributions for transgressions, and is associated with maladaptive consequences, guilt occurs when one negatively evaluates one's own self for behaving inappropriately, involves specific and temporary attributions for transgressions, and is associated with adaptive consequences (Wong &Tsai 211).

The feeling of guilt is more frequent among the members of individualistic, western societies, whereas shame is mostly felt by the members of the collectivistic cultures, such as the Iranian culture. However, Wong and Tsai continue that in collectivistic cultures a clear diction between shame and guilt is not possible:

> Shame and guilt may be less differentiated in collectivistic contexts because in these contexts people do not view themselves as separate from their relationships with others, their contexts, or their actions. Consequently, there is less emphasis placed on having an 'internal' orientation in collectivistic rather than individualistic contexts (Morling, Kitayama, & Miyamoto, 2002; Rothbaum, & Blackburn, 1984). Therefore, the differences between shame and guilt in individualistic cultures, which largely rest on this distinction, may be less pronounced in collectivistic culture (Wong & Tsai 214).

I find this hypothesis applicable to the Iranian female characters in diaspora, especially the first generation ones, as they are brought up with "collective" values. But I believe another reason why Iranian female characters of the selected works, especially the second generation characters, do not typically show one of these two emotions more strongly than the other is that their selves are formed between individualistic and collectivistic contexts as Iranians in the West. That is why in their writings shame and guilt both occur prominently.

Motlagh considers the memoir of Moaveni as an example of shame narrative as the narrator "is ashamed that she is not considered authentically Iranian by people she meets in Iran" (Motlagh 2008: 29). I should add here that this is not the only reason for the narrator's feeling of shame/guilt. She also finds herself guilty and is ashamed of her absence during and after the revolution, when those who stayed in Iran were struggling with political, economical and social changes. Referring to this issue she writes:

> There is a consensus [...] that Iranians will eventually over-
> throw this regime, and that it is simply a matter of time.
> That conviction underpinned our lives in the diaspora, and
> in its defense we saw revenge and redemption for every-
> thing we have lost.
> I had always thought that way myself, in part because I
> knew very little about post-revolutionary Iran, but more im-
> portantly, because I *wanted* it to be true. [...] It was an emo-
> tional trick to ease the pain of absence, the guilt of being
> the ones who left, or chose to stay outside. It was a delusion
> that deferred a mournful truth: that we would never regain
> the Iran before 1979, that we would never go back (Moaveni
> 37).

The narrator believes a change in the regime which takes Iran back to the relatively desirable conditions before the revolution would ease the feelings of shame and guilt among the members of Iranian Diaspora. However, as this does not seem possible, they have to live with this pain. Wong & Tsai argue that normally the feelings of guilt do not last long while shame can be a lifelong problem (211). Of course, this does not apply to the subjects who suffer from complicated guilt complexes. If they are right in their claim, the long-time inner conflict of the char- acters here should be shame, although the narrator refers to it using the word "guilt". This can be due to the incapability of the characters in differentiating between these two feelings, as I suggested above. For the narrator, however, writing is a way of overcoming her shame, as she mentions later in the memoir.

After the revolution the freedom of female subjects in Iran was lim- ited in terms of social interactions and dress code. However, the female subjects living in the Diaspora were benefiting from freedom in their new society. The comparison between these two life styles leads to feeling of shame for the some of the selected diasporic writers. In

"Captions", Layli Arbab Shirani refers to this problem in an imaginary dialogue with those who stayed:

> I grew up an Iranian, among Iranians, eating Iranian food, swallowing Iranian germs, but feeding a Western intellect that has no memory, no history, no knowledge of my suit-case. I had to overcome my shame, because it was never there, and I had to heap my suspicion on you, *your* motives —because I knew myself, because I was guilty—as we are in the West—of draping my freedom around me like a warm blanket (like a *chador?*), and incubating my ignorance (Karim 2006: 76).

The character believes that the Other, the one who stayed in Iran, is blaming her for enjoying her freedom in the West during the difficult times in Iran, without feeling guilty/ashamed.

Another reason for the guilt feeling among the narrators of the selected texts is enjoying peace in the Diaspora during Iran-Iraq war. Parisa Milani in "American Again" refers to this issue in a poetic dialogue with an Iranian Other who suffered the war.

> Will you forgive me for playing dodgeball in America
> while my brothers and sisters dodged bombs in Iran?
> Will you forgive me for loving the flag you once hated?
> Will you forgive me for deserting you?
> (Karim 2006: 220).

The narrator asks for forgiveness for not being there and also for being a citizen of the country which destroyed the lives of Iranian through war. The United States had not directly opened war against Iran, but supported Iraq in doing so, as many of the Iranians, including the poet, believe.

Also the narrator in Karim's poem "Dawn on the Fall Equinox" feels that she has betrayed her country by living in the United States during the Iran-Iraq war, a war which the United States has "unleashed". She is ashamed of caressing her son in peace while the boys in her country are being bombed.

> What those other boys
> in that place where we've unleashed
> war are thinking, I cannot say.
> Theirs is a life punctuated by
> the *ratta-tatt-tatt* of bullets,
> the mud-green of uniforms,
> and corpses of bombed-out cars.
> Waking at dim first light
> cannot be like this. Soft and sweet,
> the certainty of their mother's
> breath against neck and hair.
> In this dream-state here,
> I can only think of dressing,
> feeding him, caressing his smallness.
> [...]
> How will I explain *this* to him? In these hummed hours
> before he speaks my name,
> I pretend to have a truth
> that turns the darkness into light
> (Karim 2006: 230).

The narrator of the poem does not know how to justify her escape and betrayal to her son, when he is grown up. She is guilty in her own eyes and in those of her son. She is struggling with the individualistic feeling of guilt and the collectivistic feeling of shame at the same time.

Another reason for shame/guilt, as Asayesh refers to in her memoir, is being convinced of inferiority as an immigrant. This is a product of the marginalization she has experienced in her daily life in the Diaspora. To avoid inferiorization the character rejects relations with other Iranians. She tries to keep a distance from her compatriots to be able to integrate in the society of Americans, which is another source of shame/guilt feeling.

> I am overcome by shame. I hate myself twice, once out of the ingrained self-loathing that comes from years of being convinced of one's own inferiority, and once for the symptoms of that disease, my instinctive attempt to distance myself from my own kind (Asayesh 182).

As mentioned above, according to Fuchs writing is a means of "survival and reconciliation" and confessing can reconstruct what catastrophe has damaged." I would like to take his claim one step further and suggest that confession can also help the subject recover from the painful feelings such as shame and guilt. The authors express these feelings in autobiographical texts to make peace with both "Self" and "Other".

The narrators of the above-mentioned texts pay the price for their comfortable lives in the Diaspora during the most difficult times in Iran with feelings of shame and guilt. Confessing their feeling of shame and guilt to themselves and to the reader, they seek forgiveness. In the selected works of the female writers of Iranian diaspora it is difficult to differentiate between the personal feeling of guilt and shame which is a result of collective negative evaluations, as the characters cannot separate their individualistic selves from the collective ones. Even those who are brought up in a western culture, in which mostly guilt is contextualized, cannot avoid the feeling of shame as they are in close contact with the collectivistic Iranian culture in the diasporic community.

c. The Quest for Identity

In the selected autobiographical texts, the narrators seek for their identity through writing. In *A Passion for Difference: Essays in Anthropology and Gender* Henrietta Moore argues that autobiographical texts are based on the assumption of a singular identity, that "the author in the text and the author of the text are one and the same." However, this relationship is fictive and imaginary, shaped in language and culturally inscribed. The author in the text is the imaginary self of the author of the text, or "properly speaking, they are not two selves, but a self in process" (Moore 1994: 117-118). As Eakin in *How Our Lives Become Stories: Making Selves* puts it (the autobiographer) recognizes continuous identity not only as a fiction of memory, but also as an existential fact, necessary for psychological survival amid the flux of existence (Eakin 1999: 94).

It is through narrating the memories of her past that the character can reconstruct her shattered identity. As human beings tell and re-tell stories about their lives, they construct coherence in their accounts, enacting particular identities, as Schiffrin in "Narrative as Self-Portrait: Sociolinguistic Constructions of Identity" argues (Schiffrin 1996), and giving the teller a sense of continuity over time (Eakin 1999). However, Kraus, in "The Narrative Negotiation of Identity and Belonging", argues that narrative identity development is also a "story without closure, constantly open space to change" especially when "the creation of coherence is no longer guaranteed by the defining force of collective identities ... (but becomes) the responsibility of the individual person" (Kraus 2006: 104). Also Benstock argues in "Authorizing the Autobiography" that the search for identity in an autobiography is never-ending.

> If the autobiographical moment prepares for a meeting of 'writing' and 'selfhood', a coming together of method and subject matter, this destiny-like the retrospective glance that presumably initiates autobiography—is always deferred (Benstock 1998: 146).

Bahrampour writes of the role of remembering and retelling memories in preserving the identity of the characters. If these unique memories are forgotten, a part of their personal history and their perception of their "selves" will vanish.

> Repeating each detail, no matter how small, is a way to keep alive something that only they remember, something that would disappear forever if they did not repeat it (Bahrampour 125).

Asayesh in her memoir refers to the importance of memories, as her past and present meld in the process of remembering and she feels her identity intact again.

> The sun dazzled my eyes. The wind sang to me. The essence of my beginnings rose like sap, infusing my here-and-now with the scents of a childhood Eden. Suspended in illusion, I saw my past melding with my present. The boundaries of space and time were erased. My life felt whole (Asayesh 7).

Also Françoise Lionnet in *Postcolonial Representations* refers to the complexity and multiplicity of the of post colonial female subjects. She uses the concept of *métissage*, or cultural mixing, in her readings of a rich array of Francophone and Anglophone texts and finds it uniquely universal:

Understood as a dynamic model of relationality, I argue, *métissage* is 'universal' even if, in each specific context, power relations produce widely varying configurations, hierarchies, dissymmetries, and contradictions. [...] Women writing in postcolonial contexts show us precisely how the subject is 'multiply organized' across cultural boundaries, since this subject speaks several different languages (male and female, colonial and indigenous, global and local, among others). The postcolonial subject thus becomes quite adept at braiding all the traditions at its disposal, using the fragments that constitute it in order to participate fully in a dynamic process of transformation (Lionnet 1995: 4-5).

The memoirs under discussion have non-coherent forms which can be related to the split selves of the authors and their shattered lives. An event in daily life reminds the character of something in her past and one memory leads to the other. It is through these travels back and forth in time that the characters get to a picture of their identity. This style of writing is, however, not a typical characteristic of western autobiographies, which follow chronological order, or memoirs, which only cover a period of time in the life of the character. Maureen O'Connor in *Life Stories: A Guide to Reading Interests in Memoirs, Autobiographies, and Diaries* writes:

> The autobiography is generally seen as the purview of a person who has been in the public eye and who, toward the end of an illustrious life, sets that life down, generally in chronological order, for posterity. The memoir, in contrast, tends to be shortened in time and focuses more on the writer as an individual (O'Connor XXIII).

I believe that the form of the selected autobiographical texts here is unique and the authors have changed the genre to be able to create a non-chronological order of interlinked events which are happened in a long period of time.

Remembering is not the only method of the quest for the identity in the autobiographical works under discussion. Also dialogues with the Other, which is the continuation and reflection of self, have been made in these texts. It is through communication with the Other that the character can find the lost parts of her identity and complete the image of self.

As Milani in *Veils and Words: the Emerging Voices of Iranian Women Writers* mentions, "Writing is an attempt by women writers to establish dialogue with themselves, with other women and with men" (Milani 1992: 73). This is through writing that women make compensation between their contrasting selves in the Diaspora. They also use this medium as a means of communicating with the Other. Cixous elaborates on this issue and writes:

> Whereas subjectivity is the wealth we have in common and,

by definition, the subject is a nonclosed mix of self/s and others; the human subject who, in the Bible for example, calls himself our like. No I without you ever or more precisely no I's without you's. I is always our like. When I explore I — I take as object of observation a human sample. There is no true art which does not take as its source or root the universal regions of subjectivity (Cixous 1994: XVII).

Aphrodite Désirée Navab in "Tales Left Untold" creates a dialogue with the Other through "telling". It is in the process of telling that the character can find the silenced pieces of self and put them together:

> To tell a tale is all that's left
> To those forbidden passage home
> It's in telling
> Not the tale
> That the untold pieces get re-sewn
> To pick them up
> One
> By
> One
> And then throw them in the air
> Is this storyteller's mad hope
> That one piece will make it there
> (Karim 2006: 281)

Ann Vickery in *Leaving Lines of Gender: A Feminist Genealogy of Language Writing*, focusing on the issue of communication in writing, suggests that writing helps female writers to imagine their identity as complete and dynamic.

> Rather than a static text, writing is revealed as an action and function of communication. For many women writers, collaboration provided an imagined space in which identity could remain in flux (Vickery 2000: 249).

The narrators of the selected texts feel divided and their identities are multiple and non-coherent. They write of this situation to communicate with the '"ther" and the "self", and use the symbolism of the mirror, which is to refer not only to the illusive relation between self and the other, but also to the relation between the Imaginary and the Real. Rowbotham in *Woman's Consciousness, Man's World* argues that "The prevailing social order stands as a great and resplendent hall of mirrors. It owns and occupies the world as it is and the world as it is seen and heard" (Rowbotham 1973: 27).

The character in the poem "Perfectly Parallel Mirrors" by Laleh Khalili is experiencing a life between two mirrors, having not just one illusive image of "self", but two, or even more, as a result of living in the realm of blurring boundaries in diaspora.

Between two parallel mirrors
As if between two parts
[…]
Definition is always a precarious enterprise
In twilight—blurring boundaries—
She hunts herself in a persistence of
Mirrors and mirages and memories
The naked ambivalence of her breasts
Painted
On the interminable canvas of her lineage
And the rebellion of her navel
Reflected
On the shoulder blades of her past
Between two mirrors
As if amidst intertwined forests of fable and history
The nations persistent in her kaleidoscopic womb
(Karim 2006: 241-242).

As was mentioned earlier, the authors of the self-writings under discussion search for their identity through writing. They seek to put the parts of their shattered selves together, through retelling their memories, to get to a complete image of their identities. These travels back and forth in time make the texts non-chronological and interlinked; characteristics which are not common in the western memoirs and autobiographies. Besides, the narrators try to communicate with the "other" or their "other selves" through writing to achieve reconciliation and unification. The use of the metaphor of mirror to represent the inner dialogues is recurrent in these works.

d. Narratives about Mother Figures

Another important element in the formation of self in the selected autobiographical texts is the figure of mother. Narratives about mother figures are inseparable parts of the narratives of self as the narrators find their identities continuations of those of the mother figures. As Chodorow in *Psychoanalysis and the Sociology of Gender* claims, "the basic feminine sense of self is connected to the world, the basic masculine sense of self is separate" (Chodorow 1978: 169). She believes that female identity is the continuation of the identity of the mother. As daughters, female subjects are treated as projections of the mother, and thus never completely separate. Therefore, they define themselves as connected to others. This theory of Chodorow can justify the dominant role of mothers in the autobiographical works under discussion. The female subject who writes to find her identity, and to create a dialogue with her "self", cannot ignore her connection to the mother figure. Malin in *The Voice of the Mother: Embedded Maternal Narratives in Twentieth-Century Women's Autobiographies* claims that "Every woman autobiographer is a daughter who writes and establishes her identity through her autobiographical narrative" (Malin 2000: 1). She continues that:

> 'distinctions' between autobiography and biography, or text
> and intertext, blur, even disintegrate. The two life stories
> overlap, and the mother, the object of the biographical nar-

rative, becomes a subject, or rather an 'intersubject', in her daughter's autobiography. These texts become conversations or dialogues between a mother and a daughter (Malin 2000: 1-2).

Also Kristeva in "Women's Time" writes of the identification the female characters with the mother figure. She believes that this is not only an "imaginary potency" but also a "normative view of the social and symbolic relationship".

> This identification also bears witness to woman's desire to lift the weight of what is sacrificial in the social contract from their shoulders, to nourish our societies with a more flexible and free discourse, one able to name what has thus far never been an object of circulation in the community: the enigmas of the body, the dreams, secret joys, shames, hatreds of the second sex (Kristeva 1986: 207).

The figure of the mother is very frequent and significant in most of the literary works under discussion. In Bahrampour's memoir, the American mother with her creative and open lifestyle is a source of inspiration and power for the narrator Tara. Also the grandmother with her central role in the family provides her with an example of a successful Iranian traditional woman. Asayesh's memoir starts with the report of the return trip of Gelareh and her mother Homajoon. The mother is there to shepherd and guide the daughter. In the next chapters of the work we go back in time and read of the efforts of the mother, alongside her husband, in building a life in the diaspora for the daughters. The character Homajoon plays such an important role in this memoir that the work can be considered her biography in parts. For Moaveni, this is the aunt who plays the role of her mother during her trip to Iran. She takes care of her, introduces her to friends and the Iranian underground life of women. Although not all her advice regarding the way a woman should behave in post-revolution Iran is realistic, still the character Azadeh enjoys the security her presence provides.

As Dumas writes in the afterword of her work, it is the father who has centrality. This memoir is a satire of life in diaspora, and the behaviors of the father, as a man of wits, are good ingredients for such a work. However, this does not mean that the mother does not have a powerful role in the work, although she is mostly silent and busy with daily duties of a house wife.

In her stories the father, who is more or less integrated in the new world, has a main role. The mother, however, who has language and identity problems, is ignored by the author to a great extent. She writes:

> My mother's English prevented her from reading the book. I did, however, let her know what I had written. She gave me her blessing but had a few questions. 'Did you mention that I never left you with a babysitter, even though I could have? Did you mention that I nursed you for over two years and how difficult you were to wean? Did you mention how I was always at home when you returned from school, that you never came home to an empty house?'
>
> Although none of the above made it into the book, any mother who gives her blessing to a memoir that mocks her accent has the right to tell the world that I was a pain to wean.
>
> And this brings me to the main character in my book, my father.
>
> When I started writing my stories, I had no idea that my father would figure so prominently. Often, I would start a story about myself, and by the time I was finished, it was about my father.
>
> How this happened I do not know.
>
> (Dumas 190-191)

Throughout the memoir, the author tries to keep a distance from the traumas of immigration, through giving the humorous father, who has better language skills and a longer history of life in the Diaspora, a dominant role in the work, and ignoring the mother, who has newly joined the father in the United States and has language and integration problems. Although never mentioned clearly in the memoir, her possible intension in defining the painful moments of her mother and herself as funny can be to forget the catastrophe of integration.

Also in the poems and short prose works in the case study, one can trace the presence and importance of mother (and in cases also grandmother) in identity formation of the characters. In "The Gift" Marjan Kamali writes the story a mother who has dedicated her life to her children and weekly math sessions with her friends. She is in search of a husband for her daughter, Mina, throughout the story. Mina sees this as inacceptable and is angry about this traditional behavior of her fairly modern mother. However, it is at the end of the story that she remembers the way her father has been on her mother's side in the first difficult days of her life in the diaspora, or when she lost her mom in the war. She realizes that her mother wanted to give her daughter a husband to support her when she is not there. This is what the grandmother has also done to her daughter (Karim 2006: 183-193). Susan Atefat Pekham also writes of her mother and the way she cares about her image in the works of the daughter and the way life has changed for her. In the diaspora she is inferiorized and searches for acceptance from her daughter. But at the end we see that the narrator is also in need of the presence and words of the mother.

> Mother always had her way
> with words, squinting at my page
> to find herself, to catch my foreign
>   breath and let it linger, see it blister
> in lines and die a full death. Ey,
>   she said when I teased her
> for the hours she would spend,

for calling the flower, Gerumium,
for the way she spelled, Esnickar,
    Ey, she said, *Na Cun.* And *she*
once corrected *my* English.
[...] Nebraska wind cuts quick. I've moved
geraniums in for winter. My aching
bones long for mother's words,
dried earth, blistered lines of green.
(Karim 2006: 3-4)

Mitra Parineh in "Inheritance" tells the story of a daughter who has lost her mother as a baby and has traveled to Iran to find out more about her. Among the belongings of the mother she chooses the shoes she was wearing as she died in an accident. This may be a symbol of the will of the daughter to represent and repeat the mother. Besides, this journey is a search for her own Iranian identity, the inheritance of her mother.

They are exactly my age, gems from my mother, her foot-prints still outlined in the heel and toe of the shoes that slap like open palms on a table as the men bang, bang the dice against the *takhteh.* They are my inheritance, bought for one thousand francs in 1979 on the honeymoon when she fled, married, bred, and died in the same year. They are the only reason I have come [...] —Khaleh, Auntie, gave me piles of things that were my mother's—but the shoes are all I take with me, all I will take home besides the sound, the laughter of men, everywhere, enjoying life as they play backgammon in the basement tea-houses, late into the night, sneak brandy under their coats, share stiff drags from the *ghalyoun,* and hesitate before passing the hookah to me (Karim 2006: 44).

Also Haale in "Green World through Broken Glass" writes of the nostalgia her mother struggles with in the Diaspora and imagines her life as it has been and reflected in her belongings hidden in memory boxes:

> Mama had a shoebox for every decade
> she endured. Enough space to keep anything
> worth keeping, she'd said. Behind old vacuum parts,
>   a frayed
> curtain, she hid them-misshapen, dog-eared, bulging
> boxes I never opened. I'd just sit in front
> of their stunted tower, wondering when it struck her,
> this urge to hold, only things. Mama, with her blunt
> endings, leaving half-diced carrots on the counter,
> returning seven dinners later, no words.
> I pictured her riding open roads, trapped by burly
> men in some pool hall, dead in a ditch, or on a beach
> in daylight stopped by a seashell or by the green world
> through broken glass she decides to keep
> clenched in her fist, letting it cut, on the edge of the tide.
> (Karim 2006: 311)

Also the character of grandmother is of great importance for the writers of the works under review. Grandmother is the root and origin of the mother; she is the past, the peaceful home, the unchanged self. In "ajun" Mahru Elahi writes of her grandmother living with them in the diaspora. She is a source of comfort, although she is suffering from loneliness and fights forgetfulness.

> her hands hold mine
> the sound of tides retreating wearily through her nose
> tickling my palms she
> begins to lightly trace
> the fine lines
> anxiously awaiting her touch telling me
> my life will be long

and happy
[...]
i am losing something i never had
her stories
like flowers
curling back in on themselves.
(Karim 2006: 106-107)

Also Farnoosh Seifoddini in "Mamaan-bozorg" (Grandma) writes of the safety the grandmother would provide, even during the bombardments.

When we heard the sirens
my sisters knew what to do.
But I stood
[...] Then she would come grab me
[...] her fingertips
cold and dry
brushing my forehead
nodding
rocking
pressing my face
to a bony chest
that had nursed ten children.
I liked her huddling in the doorway with us.
(Karim 2006: 213)

As mentioned above, the mother figure is very important in the formation of the identity of the female characters of the selected works here, as they are projections and continuations of the figure of the mother. The characters identify themselves with the mother figure and writing of it results in communicating with the self. The safety felt in the presence of the Mother is reproduced in the process of recalling. The figure of mother can also be embodied by Grandmothers or aunts who have the same dominant role in the lives of the female characters.

e. Expressing Personal Social and Political Views

Writing provides the authors a chance of expressing their own social and political views. The journalistic style of writing in some of the selected texts takes the autobiographical project a step further and enables the author to give a voice to her personal views. Gilmore in *The Limits of Autobiography: Trauma and Testimony* claims that "every autobiography is the fragment of a theory" (Gilmore 2001: 12). The critiques that the writers in the diaspora express in their autobiographies represent their personal views of the two societies and political systems in which they have lived. This makes their viewpoint broader than that of writers with no migration background. Edward Said refers to this issue in *Reflections on Exile.*

> Seeing 'the entire world as a foreign land' makes possible originality of vision. Most people are principally aware of one culture, one setting, one home; exiles are aware of at least two, and this plurality of vision gives rise to an awareness of simultaneous dimensions, an awareness that—to borrow a term from music—is *contrapuntal.* (Said 2001: 186)

It is in the autobiography that the subjects can challenge inferiorization and marginalization openly, via expressing their individual understanding of the situation in Iran and in the diaspora. As Miller in *Getting Personal: Feminist Occasions and Other Autobiographical Acts* writes:

> In the face of the visible extremes of racism or misogyny, or the equally violent silences of theoretical discourses from which all traces of embodimenthave been carefully abstracted, the autobiographical project might seem a frivolous response. How can I propose a reflection about an ethicsin

criticism (an ethics requires a community) from these indi-
vidualisticgrounds? But the risk of a limited personalism, I
think, is a risk worth running— at least the movement of a
few more degrees in self-consciousness—in order to maintain an edge of surprise in the predictable margins oforgan-
ized resistances (Miller 1991: xiv).

Hornung and Ruhe in *Postcolonialism and Autobiography* see autobiography as an expedient genre for certain political purposes:

Autobiography in its widest definition seems to provide a
convenient genre to embrace the crossroad cultures from
East and West and to launch an emancipatory political and
cultural program (Hornung & Ruhe 1998: 3).

Lipstick Jihad by Azadeh Moaveni is a good example of theorizing personal views of Iranian and American culture, society and politics. Her
education as a journalist and her experience of living in the two societies enables her to provide the reader with quite comprehensive analysis of the situation. Her primary aim to travel and work in Iran (once
in 1999, and for the second time from 2000 to 2001) was to find somewhere to feel "ordinary, just like everyone else" (Moaveni 108). Motlagh claims that "Moaveni's noble decision to share the struggles of
her compatriots by living and working in Tehran earns her little re-
spect" (Motlagh 2008: 30), as she was not there after the revolution and
in time of crisis. Her autobiography with its theories is then her attempt to overcome the shame she feels for leaving her relatives and
colleagues in time of need. She tries to carry out her duties as a journalist in Iran through writing a "journalist autobiography".

The last time mass riots overran Tehran, a revolution fol-
lowed. Could it be happening all over again? Without *me*?
How could there be another revolution when I still hadn't
understood the first one? The thought that Iran might
change overnight, undergo another defining upheaval that I

would miss, was unbearable. I was naïve enough to believe I had a duty to witness history, if only as a tourist-spectator (Moaveni 35).

Writing about Iran as an American journalist, in language that did not get one banned from the country, meant effacing history from the story. It was, to read most written accounts of the political schism, as though real liberals—secular intellectuals, technocrats, and activists with no ties to the clergy—either did not exist or were too irrelevant to be counted as political realities (Moaveni 40).

The text is too subjective for a journalistic text and too theorized for an autobiography. Elahi in "Fake Farsi: Formulaic Flexibility in Iranian-American Women Writers' Memoirs." refers to this aspect of Moaveni's memoirs and believes that her work "questions the very basis of journalistic discourse: discursive lucidity that renders objective truth" (Elahi 2008: 40). Moaveni transcends the definition of the two genres in her memoir:

President Khatami, perhaps aware that recasting the state's foreign policy would be a task of Sisphyus, set about transforming the style and culture of daily life. By restructuring the upper management of Key ministries, he discreetly engineered a more relaxed official approach to Iranian's private lives. The morality police, charged with enforcing the strict social code, began to behave with less regular brutality, and the Culture Ministry issued permits for independent newspapers. In his speeches, he retired the inherited rhetoric of the revolution-martyrdom and death, struggle and enemies-and spoke instead of civil society, dialogue, and openness.

In the early years of Khatami's first term, from 1997 to 1999, Iranians experienced only modest changes. I stayed on for a few weeks, during that chaotic, life-transforming first visit, and found the atmosphere decidedly Soviet. My female relatives and I wore dark veils and sandals with socks, wiped off our lipstick when we say policeman in the distance. My aunt still came along for the ride, if a male cousin was dropping me off late at night, in case we were stoped at a checkpoint. In taxis, my relatives hissed me silent, when I jabbered critically, suggesting Tehran seemed like a giant cemetery, with nearly every street and tiny alley named for a martyr (Moaveni 40).

In "In the Gutter" Sanaz Banu Nikaein criticizes the Iranian politics which supports terrorism, as it is represented in the Western media. In her poem she also refers to the Americans' ignorance of the real life in Iran, and the marginalization of immigrants in American society.

> Yes Iran in the gutter
> when I get an American passport to travel the world
> when I deny my ancestors to get a job
> when I'd rather have American friends
> because
> because
> I see no more glamour as an Iranian
> Iranian means terrorism on TV
> Iranian means bombs in the media.
> (Karim 2006: 214)

As discussed above, some of the autobiographical works have been used as a ground for the expression of personal political and social theories by the authors. Autobiography has become a mouthpiece for the authors to criticize the conditions of life in Iran and in the Diaspora. Through this, the authors expand the limits of the autobiographical and journalistic writings. The works of these writers are standing somewhere on the threshold of the two genres: none but both at the same time.

Conclusion

As reflected in the autobiographical texts selected as the case study of this research, writing helps the female subjects preserve their psychological health through confessing their inner feelings. The effects of the trauma of migration or the catastrophes of revolution and war on the identity of the female characters in the Diaspora form a main part of these works. The project of writing is also a quest for identity. Furthermore, stories of the mother figures and motherhood are frequently mentioned in the selected works. Besides, narratives of guilt and shame are included in these works as the characters blame themselves/ are blamed for leaving their country and people in difficult times and enjoyed peace and freedom in the West. The feelings of shame and guilt, which are rooted in public and private domains, cannot be differentiated here, due to the collective and/or in-between selves of the characters. A journalistic style is also used in these works to fight the inferiorization in the diaspora and expressing personal social and political theories.

CHAPTER FIVE: CONCLUSION

Summing Up

As mentioned above, in the last 50 years many Iranians left the country for the West in search of freedom and knowledge. There are several literary works written by the Iranians in the Diaspora. The early works of the female writers are more political and social, while the more recent ones focus on the identity issues of the characters. There have been few researches carried out on the late literary works and memoirs of Iranian female writers in the Diaspora. In this research this literary practice has been introduced and analysed using the post-colonial and post-modern theories of space, bilingualism, autobiography and gender.

The Chapter, "Space and Gender", includes three subtitles of *Home and Gender, City and Gender,* and *Homeland and Gender.* Under *Home and Gender* I discussed the association of women with cyclical, ahistorical time/space of home and reference to home as a place of refuge and of origin, as mentioned in the case study. In the section *City and Gender,* urban life and gender in both Iranian cities and western cities, has been examined. Female characters of the mentioned works have the obstacles of gender segregation, religion and limited freedom in Iranian cities and towns. On the other hand, these cities provide them with constant communication, facilitating the sense of belonging. However, contact with the values of "globalized space" through media has led to the development of an underground life in the Iranian cities in recent years, as is reflected in some of the selected literary works. Besides, in Western cities female characters experience freedom due to the density and anonymity. Also they have to face a lack of communication and marginality in the new urban life. All these issues form and affect the gendered identity of the characters. In the last part of this chapter, *Homeland and Gender,* I discussed the significance of Iranian cultural identity for the female characters. They play an important role in the creation of an "Imaginary Homeland" in the Diaspora through observing Iranian traditions and practicing rituals. I argued that women have an important role in the preservation of the collective identity of the community of Iranians in the diaspora as markers of insider/outsider boundaries and transmitting it to the next generation.

The chapter "Bilingualism and Gender" includes the two sections on *Second Language Acquisition and Gender* and *Writing in the Language of the Other.* Here I have used the theories of bilingualism, gender and Diaspora to analyze the condition of female characters in the selected works of Iranian female writers in the Diaspora. Second language learning differs from one generation of female characters to the other, as their investment in language, educational background and gendered roles varies. Under *Writing in the Language of the Other* I have discussed the creation of personal English and using English as the language of taboos and secrets, as reflected in the case study.

The chapter "Writing and Gender", includes the two sections of *Iranian Women and Writing* and *Autobiographical works of the Second Generation of Iranian Female Writers in the Diaspora.* Post-colonial theories of autobiography and identity has been applied to analyse the texts here. Under the first subtitle, I have given a brief survey of the tradition of autobiographical writing by Iranian women in Iran and in the Diaspora. Autobiography writing of women has not been common in Iran. In the Diaspora, however, autobiography became one of the main genres of the literary productions of Iranian female authors. The first generation autobiographers in the diaspora focused mostly on their social and political lives. On the other hand, the autobiographies of the second generation authors reflect their personal lives and their identity crises. In the other section I studied the main themes of these works including victim stories, narratives of shame, quest for identity, narratives about mother figures and expressing personal theories.

Findings

Although post-modern and post-colonial theories have contributed greatly to the investigation of Diaspora literature, little has been done on Iranian Diaspora literature. The most recent memoirs and literary works of Iranian female writers in the Diaspora have been barely studied using such theories. Here a selection of these works has been analyzed using the post-modern and post-colonial theories of space, bilingualism, autobiography and gender so that the gap in the knowledge regarding the form and content of the mentioned literary practice is filled.

In this research, the significance of home, city, homeland and global spaces in the formation of the identity of female characters has been analyzed in selected works of Iranian women living in the Diaspora, using post-colonial and post-modern theories of Space and Gender.

Home is a space of refuge from history where identity is protected. Displacement from home leads to detachment from the self. Female subjects are in a quest to regain or remember their homes, where they felt absolute and belonged. The mother figure is associated with this space as the preserver of the value system of it. The female characters of the selected works are expected by the community of Iranians in the Diaspora to be fixed and unchanging in terms of identity and values, like the mental image of the mother and the home they are connected with. Home is the territory of women in the gender segregated society of Iran, reported by the narrators of the selected literary works. It is in this space that women could get together and socialize in close physical contact, which would be inacceptable in the western value system.

Another aspect of this chapter is the analysis of the gendered identity of Iranian female characters of these works who live in Iranian cities. These cities are reflected as spaces where tradition and religion govern the lives of the characters. The gendered access to the public spaces and the obligatory hijab in Iranian cities has led to the isolation and depression of some of the female characters of the first generation after the revolution. However, following the traditional norms of these cities leads to a feeling of safety among some characters. The religious spaces are among the few spaces where women have freedom of access in Iranian cities. Therefore, visiting these spaces is a social experience rather than a religious one for some characters. Still, the characters who are in permanent contact with such spaces start to develop religious views such as fear of the wrath of God or belief in fate. They may even tend to superstitious ideas such as fearing the "evil eye".

Although the close relations between people are appreciated in some cases, there are also references to the restrictions the characters feel in the dense social structure that these urban spaces provide. Some of the female characters of these works experience a clash between local Muslim values and globalized secular values in Iranian cities. So a hybrid code of behavior and belief is formed among them. A feeling of dissatisfaction with the present situation is always with the characters, as a consequence of globalization. Due to the flow of technology and media transferring western values, the characters feel unsatisfied and unwilling to accept their own cultural values. The sexuality and aesthetic values of the characters become problematic and the characters try to create an underground globalized space to overcome the limitations they face in their social life in Iranian cities. Still, there are characters who stick to the traditional and religious values to prevent the "loss of self".

Modern western cities, due to the density and anonymity that makes freedom possible, are quite different from the smaller Iranian towns and cities where people have still preserved their traditions and limit themselves in their social and personal lives. For some of the female characters this freedom is favorable, although the community of Iranians tries to control women, as the preservers of the value system of the community. The families and the community limit the access of the female characters to specific public space to avoid the transformation of their sexual and gendered values. However, such a transformation is mostly an inevitable consequence of life in western cities. On the other hand, some female characters in these works sustain a fundamentalist view of freedom and sexual values, and try to spread their ideas in the community to preserve their national identity in the Diaspora.

Besides, although for some female characters in these works privacy and social and religious freedom in a western city is desirable, but the unbridgeable distance between people and anonymity in the vast western cities are not acceptable. Iranian female characters in these works have got used to being in close relations with others and little privacy during their lives in Iranian cities. Therefore, the characters try to create an Iranian city in the hostland, a Tehrangeles in Los Angeles, where the social interactions and values resembles those back home.

As narrated in literary productions of the Iranian female writers in the Diaspora, displacement from the space of homeland affects the gendered and sexual identity of the characters. In some cases, the characters travel back to Iran to reunify with their national identity. However, they mostly find their homeland changed, due to the flow of the values of the globalized world through media and technology. They have a feeling of perpetual homelessness and cannot find a homeland to associate themselves with. Therefore, they create an "imaginary homeland" for themselves by forming a society of co-patriots in their surroundings, to avoid identity problems and nostalgia. This new homeland in the diaspora gives them a feeling of being at their "real" homeland, a sense of completeness in terms of identity. This parallel imagined space is not a homeland still, but a resistance method against the feeling of being rootless. Female characters play an important role in the formation and preservation of this imagined space. It is their duty to observe the national values and transfer them to the next generation. Sexuality of the female characters defines the boundaries between self and other, national and foreign.

As young adults, however, the second generation characters try to integrate themselves in their new society and avoid the in-between life and identity of their parents. This includes the rejection of their Irani-anness. But as adults they achieve reconciliation with their Iranian national identity, as they overcome their need to belong in the host land. They live in a third space, which is a mixture of symbols from past and elements from the globalized world they live in. So the characters are both Iranian and western, and at the same time, neither Iranian nor western.

In discussing bilingualism and cultural identity in the Diaspora the ideas of Norton, among others, have be applied to texts to clarify the way bilingualism affects the lives of Iranian women in diaspora. The investment of the female characters in language is different among the two generation of diasporic characters. In case of first generation characters, lack of interest in language acquisition as an identity defense method, lack of basic education which facilitates language acquisition, and lack of enough contact with new society and language as house-wives, are the issues I could find out in the selected literary works. However, second generation characters have a great interest in language acquisition due to their integrative motivation. Finally, the use of language by Iranian female writers in diaspora as resistance against dominant language and culture of the hostland has been explored.

One of the main questions of the chapter "Writing and Gender" is the function of writing in the lives of the narrators of the literary texts under discussion. I have argued that autobiographical writing by women is a therapy and defense method against the traumas of revolution, war, and migration. Confessing their pains through writing helps the narrators in reconciliation with their past. Also narratives of shame/guilt are included in these works as the female characters feel guilty because of leaving for the West when their country and people needed them more than ever. They are ashamed of having enjoyed peace and freedom in the West while their compatriots in Iran where suffering from war, revolution or social pressures and through writing try to make peace with themselves and the reader. Feelings of shame and guilt are used interchangeably in these works as the characters cannot separate their private feelings, such as guilt, from the collective ones, including shame. This is due to their collective and/or in-between identities as the members of Iranian diaporic community. Autobiography is also a safe ground for the narrator to put the pieces of her shattered identity together so as to reach a more complete picture of the self. However, this is an endless quest, as the narrator's identity is multiple and hybrid. Remembering the times before the Iranian identity was transformed due to life in the diaspora has great significance for the identity of the narrators. Also a dialogue with the other or self is frequently included in these texts, showing the urge of the narrator to communicate and to make a bridge between her two identities. In the autobiographical works under discussion, the mother figure plays an important role, as the characters experience themselves as the continuation of this figure and writing about it leads to the unification with their lost self. Another main theme of some of these works is the presentation of personal theories of the authors regarding social life and political conditions in Iran and in the Diaspora. In their writings they take a step towards the creation of the hybrid genre of journalistic autobiography.

APPENDIX I
SELECTED BIBLIOGRAPHY OF THE LITERARY WORKS OF IRANIAN WOMEN IN THE DIASPORA

Amirrezvani, Anita. *The Blood of Flowers: A novel*. New York: Back Bay Books, 2008. Print.

—. *Equal of the sun*. 1st Scribner trade pbk. ed. New York: Scribner, 2013, c2012. Print.

Amirrezvani, Anita, and Persis M. Karim. *Tremors: New fiction by Iranian American writers*. 2013. Print.

Andalibian, Rahimeh. *The Rose Hotel: A memoir of secrets, loss, and love from Iran to America*. 2015. Print.

Ansary, Nina. *Jewels of Allah: The untold story of women in Iran*. 2015. Print.

Asayesh, Gelareh. *Saffron Sky: A life between Iran and America*. Boston, Mass: Beacon Press, 1999. Print.

Azam Zanganeh, Lila. *My sister, guard your veil; my brother, guard your eyes: Uncensored Iranian voices*. Boston, Mass: Beacon Press, 2006. Print.

Bahrampour, Tara. *To see and see again: A life in Iran and America*. 1st pbk. ed. Berkeley: University of California Press, 2000. Print.

Bijan, Donia. *Maman's homesick pie: A Persian heart in an American kitchen*. Chapel Hill, N.C: Algonquin Books of Chapel Hill, 2011. Print.

Dehdashi, Catherine. *Channeling Iran, Bridging Cultures: Food, Memory, and the Search for Self and Home in Iranian-American Women's Memoirs*: Create Space Independent Publishing Platform, 2013. Print.

Diba, Farah. *An Enduring Love*. New York, N.Y: Miramax, 2004. Print.

Dumas, Firoozeh. *Laughing without an accent: Adventures of an Iranian American, at home and abroad.* 2009 Random House trade paperback ed. New York: Random House Trade Paperbacks, 2009. Print.

—. *Funny in Farsi: A memoir of growing up Iranian in America.* New York: Random House Trade Paperbacks, 2004. Print.

Fathi, Nazila. *The lonely war: One woman's account of the struggle for modern Iran.* New York, Basic Books: 2014. Print.

Fotouhi, Sanaz. *Literature of the Iranian diaspora: Meaning and identity since the Islamic revolution.* London, New York: I.B. Tauris, 2015, cop. 2015. Print. Written culture and identity 5.

Ḥakkākiyān, Ru'yā. *Journey from the land of no: A girlhood caught in revolutionary Iran.* New York, Enfield: Random House; Hi Marketing [distributor], 2006. Print.

—. *Assassins of the Turquoise Palace.* 1st ed. New York: Grove Press, 2011. Print.

Jasmine and Stars: Reading More Than Lolita in Tehran: Univ of North Carolina Pr, 2009. Print.

Karim, Persis M. *A world between: Poems, short stories, and essays by Iranian-Americans.* 1st ed. New York: Braziller, 1999. Print.

—. *Let me tell you where I've been: New writing by women of the Iranian diaspora.* Fayetteville: University of Arkansas Press, 2006. Print.

Mehran, Marsha. *Rosewater and soda bread: A novel.* New York: Random House Trade Paperbacks, 2008. Print.

—. *Pomegranate soup: A novel.* New York: Random House Trade Paperbacks, 2006. Print.

Moaveni, Azadeh. *Lipstick jihad: A memoir of growing up Iranian in America and American in Iran.* Princeton, N.J: Recording for the Blind & Dyslexic, 2006. Print.

—. *Honeymoon in Tehran: Two years of love and danger in Iran.* Random House Trade pbk. ed. New York: Random House, 2010. Print.

Nafisi, Azar. *Reading Lolita in Tehran: A memoir in books.* Random House deluxe trade pbk. ed. 2008. Print.

—. *The republic of imagination: America in three books.* The Viking Press; 1st edition. 2014. Print.

—. *Things I've been silent about: Memories of a prodigal daughter.* Random House trade pbk. ed. New York: Random House Trade Paperbacks, 2010, c2008. Print.

Nahai, Gina B. *The luminous heart of Jonah S.* Akashic Books, 2014. Print.

Navai, Ramita. *City of lies: Love, sex, death, and the search for truth in Tehran.* First edition. UK: Weidenfeld & Nicolson, 2014. Print.

Pahlavi, Ashraf. *Faces in a mirror: Memoirs from exile.* Englewood Cliffs, N.J: Prentice-Hall, 1980. Print.

Satrapi, Marjane. *Chicken with plums.* 1st American ed. New York: Pantheon Books, 2006. Print.

—. *The complete Persepolis.* 1st ed. New York: Pantheon Books, 2007. Print.

—. *Embroideries.* London: J. Cape, 2008. Print.

—. *The Sigh.* Los Angeles, Calif: Archaia Entertainment LLC, 2011. Print.

Seraji, Mahbod. *Rooftops of Tehran.* New York, NY: New American Library, 2009. Print.

Sofer, Dalia. *The Septembers of Shiraz.* New York: Harper Perennial, 2008. Print.

Soomekh, Saba. *From the Shahs to Los Angeles: Three generations of Iranian Jewish women between religion and culture.* New York: State University of New York, 2013. Print.

Varzi, Roxanne. *Warring souls: Youth, media, and martyrdom in post-revolution Iran.* Durham N.C.: Duke University Press, 2006. Print.

Wilcox-Ghanoonparvar, Tara. *Hyphenated identities: Second-generation Iranian-Americans speak.* Costa Mesa, Calif: Mazda Publishers, 2007. Print.

APPENDIX II
SHORT BIOGRAPHIES
OF THE AUTHORS OF THE CASE STUDY

Azin Arefi was born in Iran and moved to the United States when she was a child. She studied English literature at the University of California, Berkeley, and received her master's in creative writing at UC Davis. She teaches English literature and creative writing at De Anza College in Cupertino, California, and at San Jose City College. Her fiction has been included in a number of publications, such as the online literary magazine *The Iranian, Berkeley Test, A Light Left On*, and *Spice (Stories on Stage Davis)*.[1] She is also the author of *Stories in Pictures* published by University of California, Davis (2002).

Gelareh Asayesh was born in Iran and moved to the United States before the Islamic Revolution of Iran. She has published a novel entitled *Saffron Sky: A Life Between Iran and America* (1999). She served as a journalist for the *Miami Herald* and the *Baltimore Sun* and wrote articles for *Boston Globe, the Washington Post, St. Petersburg Times,* and National Public Radio. (Karim 2006: 339)

Susan Atefat-Peckham was born in 1970 to Iranian parents in New York City. As a child, she lived in France and went to boarding school across the border in Switzerland. She attended Baylor University in Waco, Texas. She majored in biology and chemistry and got a master's degree in English. In 1999 she received her Ph.D. at the University of

---

1   I used the MLA 7 citation style to organize the quotations in this work. According to this style, in the parenthetical citations for sources from internet the name of the website or the title of the text should be used, in case the name of the author of the source is not mentioned. There is no need to give paragraph or page numbers. The citation corresponds to the first item that appears in the Work Cited entry.

Nebraska-Lincoln, where she taught creative writing, literature, and composition. Her nonfiction manuscript *Black Eyed Bird* was a finalist in the Associated Writing Programs Intro Award, and her poetry collection *That Kind of Sleep* was published in 2001 by Coffee House Press. Her work was included in the anthology *In the Field of Words*, published by Prentice-Hall in 2001, and her works appeared in *Borderlands, Texas Poetry Review, The International Poetry Review, International Quarterly, The Literary Review, The MacGuffin, Northwest Review, Onthebus, Prairie Schooner, Puerto Del Sol, The Southern Poetry Review, The Sycamore Review*, and *The Texas Review*. She taught Creative Writing at Hope College in Holland, Michigan. She was the co-founding editor of the *Milkwood Review*, an online literary journal. In 2002, she began a position at George College and State University as Poetry Editor for *Arts and Letters*, a literary journal, as well as teaching. On February 7, 2004, she died in an auto accident in Amman, Jordan. (*Peckham*)

Tara Bahrampour was the child of a mixed, Iranian and American couple. Her memoir *To See and See Again: A Life in Iran and America* is published by Farrar, Straus and Giroux in 1999. Her work appeared in the *New Yorker,* the *New York Times*, the *American Scholar*, the *New Republic,* and other journals. She works as a writer at the *Washington Post.* (Karim 2006: 340)

Layla Dowlatshahi graduated from UC Berkeley and received her MFA from Goddard College. *Joys of Lipstick* was staged at The Producer's Club and was written up in *The New York Times. Waiting Room* had a staged reading at the Annenberg Studio Theatre at the University of Pennsylvania. She has completed three additional plays, (*Waiting Room* and *Joys of Lipstick* are slated to be published by Temple University Press) a teleplay and a novel, *Stones in the Garden.* She teaches writing at Normandale Community College Bloomington, MN United States. (*Normandale AFA*)

Firoozeh Dumas was born in Abadan, Iran, and moved to California at the age of seven. After a two-year stay, she and her family moved back to Iran and resided in Ahvaz and Tehran. Two years later, Dumas returned to California, where she later attended the University of California at Berkeley. *Funny in Farsi* is her first book. The book was a finalist for both the PEN/USA Award in 2004 and the Thurber Prize for American Humor, and has been adopted in junior high, high school and college curricula throughout the nation. It has been selected for common reading programs at several universities. Dumas is also the author of *Laughing Without an Accent,* a collection of autobiographical essays published in May 2008. (*Firoozehdumas.com*)

Mahru Elahi is a writer and zine-maker living in San Francisco. She recently had several pages of her zine "Riding Rough Roads Really Slow" published in the anthology *Days I Moved Through Ordinary Sounds* (2015). She has taught literary arts for a decade and received her Master of Science in Teaching at New School University in New York City. Her non-fiction and poetry have appeared in several magazines and journals. (*City*)

Parinaz Eleish is an Iranian-born painter and poet living in Massachusetts. She completed her master's degree in film at Boston University and also obtained a master's degree in writing from the University of New Hampshire. (*Khaki Gallery*)

Amanda Enayati is an attorney, a columnist, author, and speaker whose essays about stress, happiness, creativity, technology, and identity have appeared on CNN, PBS, NPR, *Washington Post, Reader's Digest, Salon,* etc. Born in Tehran, she fled the Iranian revolution as a child and lived in several countries before settling in the United States in the mid-1980s. (*Enayati*)

Farnaz Fatemi is an Iranian American poet and freelance writer living in Santa Cruz, California. She teaches writing at UC Santa Cruz. Her work is included in the anthology *Love and Pomegranates: Artists and Wayfarers on Iran* published by Nortia Press Nuttal Sayres (2013). (*Perihelion*)

Tara Fatemi Walker was a UCSC student in Santa Cruz. She has lived in Northern California, Los Angeles, San Francisco and Austin. She returned to Santa Cruz in 2004. She writes about identity and belonging. Besides, she writes about food, restaurants, and culinary events. (Karim 2006: 341) (*Santa Cruz Life*)

Elham Gheytanchi was born and raised in Tehran. She teaches sociology in Santa Monica College (CA, USA). She holds a BA (1995) and MA (1998) in sociology from UCLA. She received her Ph.D in sociology program from UCLA in 2001. Her master's thesis entitled "Civil Society in Iran: Politics of Motherhood and Public Sphere" was published in *International Sociology Journal*, (2001). Her other publications include "Frauen in der Islamischen Öffentlichkeit in Iran", in *Islam in Sicht: Der Auftritt von Muslimen im öffentlichen Raum* (2004), and "Chronology of Events Regarding Women in Iran since the Revolution of 1979" in *Social Research Journal* (2000). She has also written literary reviews on Iranian contemporary literature, published in *Persian Book Review Journal, Karnameh,* and *The Iranian.* She has also worked as a consultant to several broadcasting companies and radio programs in US and Europe. (*The Iranian*)

Haale is the artistic name of Haale Gafori. She is an Iranian-American singer, composer, and poet who lives in New York City. She was born in the Bronx, to Persian parents. Her music has been described as "Psychedelic Sufi Trance Rock". She sings original lyrics in English as well as excerpts of Persian poetry by poets like Rumi and Sohrab Sepehri in Persian. (*Peyvand*)

Zjaleh Hajibashi was born in Denton, Texas. She received a B.A. in English Literature from Rice University and has a Master's Degree in Persian Literature and a PhD in Comparative Literature from the University of Texas. She attended the Persian Program at the University of Virginia in Fall 2000. Her articles on Persian literature and her reviews have appeared in *Critique, Edebiyat, Iranian Studies, Journal of Middle East Studies,* and *Middle East Report.* Some of her works are also included in the anthology *A World Between* (Karim 1999). (*University of Virginia*)

Roya Hakakian is the author of *Journey from the Land of No* (2004), a memoir of growing up as a Jewish teenager in post-revolutionary Iran, as well as two collections of poetry, including *For the Sake of Water.* She currently serves as an editorial board member of World Affairs. She writes for numerous publications like the *New York Times, Wall Street Journal* and NPR's *All Things Considered.* She is a founding member of the Iran Human Rights Documentation Center. (*Hakakian*)

Haleh Hatami lives in Oakland, California. Her Poetry and essays have been published in *Phoebe, FO A RM,* and *Chain.* Her translations of the poems of Iranian poet, Yadollah Royaee appeared in *26* and in *Strange Times My Dear: the Pen Anthology of Contemporary Iranian Literature.* She has received the CPIC Life Poetry Award from San Francisco State University and the Ann Fields Poetry Award. She has written for Golden Thread Productions Theater Company. (*Kenyon Review*)

Taraneh Hemami was born and raised in Tehran, Iran, and living and working in San Francisco. She is an installation artist and painter and received her MFA from the California College of the Arts (in Oakland) in 1991. Since then she has exhibited her work locally and internationally. Besides being the 2006 artist-in-residence at CCA, she is the director of *Hall of Reflections,* a collaborative art project that gathers and displays the stories and photographs of the Bay Area Iranian diaspora community. Her latest exhibition is entitled *Fabrications: Theory of Survival*, curated installation at Southern Exposure, San Francisco, in 2014. (*Hemami*)

Zara Houshmand is an Iranian-American writer who was raised in the Philippines. She has received her BA in English Literature from London University. Her recent book is *A Mirror Garden* (2007), co-authored with Monir Shahroudy Farmanfarmaian. Her poetry has been published in anthologies including *A World Between* (Karim 1999) and in journals such as *Caesura, Persian Book Review, West Coast Line, Di-verse-city*, and *Texas Observer*. Her play *The Future Ain't What It Used to Be* was staged at the Burbage Theatre in Los Angeles (1986). She received the first commissioning grant from the National Theatre Translation Fund for her translations from Persian which have been published in several journals and anthologies including *Literature from the Axis of Evil* (2006), *Words Without Borders* (2007) and *Strange Times, My Dear: The PEN Anthology of Contemporary Iranian Literature* (2006).(*Words Without Borders*)

Niloofar Kalaam grew up in Tehran. She holds degrees in engineering, mathematics and clowning. Her poetry and essays have been published in *Shahrvand, Peace Magazine*, and the *Iranian Times*. She lives in Toronto. (Karim 2006: 342)

Marjan Kamali was born in Turkey to Iranian parents in 1971 and moved to Forest Hills, Queens, in 1982. She has also lived in Germany, Kenya and Switzerland. She holds a degree in English literature from UC Berkeley, a master's in business administration from Columbia University, and a master's in creative writing from New York University. Her creative writing thesis entitled "Together Tea", published by Ecco in 2013. In 2004 she moved to Sydney, Australia. (*Boston Athenæum*)

Esther Kamkar was born in Iran in 1947 and came to the United States in 1972 after a seven-year stay in Jerusalem. She received an Artist Grant from the Peninsula Community Foundation (2001) to publish a collection of her poetry, *Hummingbird Conditions* and a grant from the Clay and Glass Arts Foundation (2003) for her project, "Personal Narratives in Poetry and Clay". Her books include *Hum of Bees* (2011), *Hummingbird Conditions* (2002), published by Ziba Press, and *Chapbook A Leopard in My Pocket* (1998). She lives and works in California. (*Kamkar*)

Persis M. Karim was born and raised in the San Francisco Bay Area by her Iranian father and French mother. She is contributing author and editor of three anthologies of literature; *Tremors: New Fiction by Iranian American Writers* (2013), *Let Me Tell You Where I've Been: New Writing by Women of the Iranian Diaspora* (2006) both published by the University of Arkansas Press, and *A World Between: Poems Short Stories and Essays by Iranian Americans*, published by George Braziller, Inc. (1999). She teaches literature and creative writing at San Jose State University. (*Persiskarim.com*)

Firoozeh Kashani-Sabet received her B.A. from the University of North Carolina at Chapel Hill, where she was a Morehead Scholar. She completed her M.A., M.Phil., and Ph.D. in history at Yale University. Her book, *Frontier Fictions: Shaping the Iranian Nation, 1804-1946*, Princeton University Press (1999), was translated into Persian by Kitabsara Press, Tehran, Iran. Her other book is entitled *Conceiving Citizens: Women and the Politics of Motherhood in Iran*, Oxford University Press (2011), which received the 2012 book award from the *Journal of Middle East Women's Studies*. She has written several fictional works. Her first novel, *Martyrdom Street,* was published by Syracuse University Press in 2010. She has directed the Middle East Center at the University of Pennsylvania since 2006. (*University of Pennsylvania*)

Laleh Khalili was born in Iran and moved to the United States in 1985, in the age of sixteen. She has received her BSc at the University of Texas and her MPhil and PhD at the University of Columbia. She is a lecturer in politics at the School of Oriental and African Studies, University of London. Her first book, *Heroes and Martyrs of Palestine: The Politics of National Commemoration,* Cambridge (2007), is an ethnographic research in the Palestinian refugee camp of Burj al-Barajna in Lebanon. She also edited *Modern Arab Politics,* Routledge (2008), and co-edited (with Jillian Schwedler) *Policing and Prisons in the Middle East: Formations of Coercion,* Hurst/OUP (2010). Her most recent book is *Time in the Shadows: Confinement in Counterinsurgencies,* Stanford (2013), which was the winner of the Susan Strange Best Book Prize of the British International Studies Association and the 2014 best book award of the International Political Sociology section of the ISA. (*SOAS, University of London*)

Mimi Khalvati was born in Tehran and grew up on the Isle of Wight. She has studied at Drama Centre London and worked as an actor in the UK and as a director at the Theatre Workshop Tehran. Her pamphlet, *Persian Miniatures,* published by Smith/Doorstop (1990) was a winner of the Poetry Business competition 1989. Her collections include *In White Ink* (1991), *Mirrorwork* (1995), *Entries on Light* (1997), *The Chine* (2002), *The Meanest Flower* (2007), *Child: New and Selected Poems 1991–2011.* Her most recent collection is *The Weather Wheel.* She is the founder of The Poetry School and has co-edited its anthologies, *Tying the Song* (2000), *Entering the Tapestry* (2003) and *I Am Twenty People!* (2007), published by Enitharmon Press. She is a tutor for The Poetry School and a freelance creative writing teacher. (*Khalvati*)

Nika Khanjani is Iranian born and a writer, activist and video-artist. She has created the video art piece *Neither Here Nor There: A Study of an Adopted City,* which takes the viewer into the urban and social spaces that fascinated the artist at her arrival to Montreal. (*Montréal, arts interculturels*)

Michelle Koukhab teaches English and creative writing in Los Angeles. In 2001, she received her MFA in poetry from the University of Maryland. She was a waiter at the Bread Loaf Writers' Conference in 2005. (Karim 2006: 344)

Mojdeh Marashi is a writer, translator, artist and designer. Her work is deeply influenced by the ancient and modern history of Iran. She was born in Tehran and moved to the San Francisco Bay Area in 1977. She studied at California College of Arts (CCA) and later at San Francisco State University where she earned her M.A. in Interdisciplinary Arts and an M.A. in Creative Writing. (*Smashwords*)

Parissa Milani was born in Iran and moved to the US at an early age. She received her BA in English at San Jose State University, and an MFA in creative writing at San Francisco State University. (Karim 2006: 344)

Azadeh Moaveni was born in California before the Islamic Revolution of 1979 (*Lipstick Jihad*). She earned her degree in politics at UC Santa Cruz. She has also studied Arabic at the American University in Cairo (Karim 2006: 344). She has written for *Time, The New York Times Book Review, The Washington Post*, NPR, and the *Los Angeles Times.* She is the author of *Lipstick Jihad: A Memoir of Growing up Iranian in America and American in Iran* (2005) and coauthor, with Nobel Peace Prize laureate Shirin Ebadi, of *Iran Awakening: A Memoir of Revolution and Hope* (2006) (*Goodreads Author*). Her last book is entitled *Honeymoon in Tehran: Two Years of Love and Danger in Iran*, published by Random House (2009).

Leyla Momeny has studied philosophy at UCLA. Her research interests are photography and cultural studies (Karim 2006: 345). Her poems have appeared in *The Iranian* and her non-fiction prose in *OCWeekly*.

Farnoosh Moshiri has published plays, short stories, and translations in Iranian literary magazines before the 1979 revolution and in anthologies outside Iran in the 1980s. In 1983, she left Iran and lived in refugee camps for four years before emigrating to the U.S. in 1987. Her novels and collections include *At the Wall of Almighty* (1999), *The Bathhouse* (2001, 2002), *The Crazy Dervish and the Pomegranate Tree* (2004), and *Against Gravity* (2006). She has received the *Florida Review*'s creative non-fiction award, the Barthelme Memorial Award, the Barbara Deming Award, two consecutive Black Heron Awards for Social Fiction, and the Valiente Award from Voices Breaking Boundaries. She has taught playwriting, literature, and creative writing at the Universities of Tehran, Kabul, Houston, and Syracuse. Her new novel, *Drum Tower* is published in 2014 by Sandstone Press. (*Moshiri*)

Beatrice Motamedi is the daughter of a French mother and an Iranian father. She was born in Paris and went to the United States via Canada when she was seven years old. She studied at Northwestern University and joined the Stegner Program in Creative Writing at Stanford. She has been a reporter for the *San Francisco Chronicle*, and her work is published in *Newsweek, Health,* and *Salon.com* (Karim 2006:345)

Amy Motlagh received her PhD in Near Eastern Studies at Princeton University. Born to an American mother and Iranian father, she was 2 years old when her family left Iran for San Diego just months before the Revolution. She is a professor of English and comparative literature at the American University in Cairo and the author of *Burying the Be-*

loved: Marriage, Realism, and Reform in Modern Iran (2011). (*Pomona College Magazine*)

Aphrodite Désirée Navab is an artist and writer who lives in New York City. She is of Iranian and Greek descent. In 2004 she received an Ed.D doctorate in Art Education at Columbia University. Her doctoral dissertation is published as *De-Orientalizing Iran: The Art of Sevruguin, Neshat, Navab, and Ghazel* by Lampert Academic Publishing (2011). She received her BA in Visual and Environmental Studies from Harvard College in 1993. Her art has been displayed in more than one hundred exhibitions and is included in several permanent collections such as: the Lowe Art Museum, the Harn Museum of Fine Arts, Casoria Contemporary Art Museum, Naples, Italy, and the Museum of Fine Arts, Arkansas State University. Her writing is published in a number of anthologies including *Photographic Theory: An Historical Anthology* (2014), edited by Andrew Hershberger, UK: Wiley Black-well, and *POWWOW: Charting the Fault Lines in the American Experience, Short Fiction from Then to Now* (2009), edited by Ishmael Reed. She was Assistant Professor of Art at the University of Florida and Area Coordinator of the BFA and MFA creative photography programs (2003–4). She also taught at The School of Visual Arts (2008-9). (*Navab*)

Negin Neghabat was born in Tehran in 1979 and grew up in Germany. She moved to the United States to attend university. She earned a BA in international business at San Diego State University and received an MBA at the University of Chicago. She works in corporate marketing. (Karim 2006: 346)

Sanaz Banu Nikaein studied in UC Berkeley. She is an attorney in California. She was appointed president of the International First Aid Society in 2003. She also worked as the campaign manager for Badi Badiozamani, a candidate for California governor. (Karim 2006: 346)

Mitra Parineh was born in California. Her parents were Iranian immigrants. She received her BA and MA in English at San Jose State University and holds an MFA in fiction. (Karim 2006: 346) She is currently Professor in the Writing department at University of Southern California, Los Angeles, CA. (*University of Southern California*)

Sharon L. Parker received a PhD in 2005 in the Comparative Cultural and Comparative Literary Studies Program at the University of Arizona. Her dissertation focuses on contemporary Iranian women artists. She moved in 1958 to Iran and lived there for nine years, returning in 1976 and 2001. She has been an assistant professor in the Department of Art and Design at Zayed University in Abu Dhabi, United Arab Emirates. (Karim 2006: 346)

PAZ is the pen name of Iranian American performance artist "Dirty Phoenix". Her writing and performance explores the boundaries and layers of the identity and experience of modern Iranian American female. She had a comedy show called *The Asses of Evil* in New York City. (*Labyrinth Books*)

Nasrin Rahimieh is Howard Baskerville Professor of Humanities, Comparative Literature School of Humanities, University of California. In 1988, she received her PhD at University of Alberta in Comparative Literature. Her publications include *Oriental Responses to the West: Comparative Essays on Muslim Writers from the Middle East* by Brill (1990) and *Missing Persians: Discovering Voices in Iranian Cultural Heritage* by Syracuse University Press (2001). Her reviews and articles have been published in *Iranian Studies, Comparative Literature Studies, Iran Nameh, The Middle East Journal, The Comparatist, Thamyris, Edebiyat, International Journal of Middle East Studies, Canadian Literature,* and *New Comparison. (UC Irvine, Rahimieh)*

Farnoosh Seifoddini holds an MFA in creative writing from San

Francisco State University. Her poetry has been published in the *North American Review*, the *Kennesaw Review*, and *Transfer Magazine*. She has received the Ann Fields Poetry Prize and the Mark Linenthal Poetry Prize and has been a finalist for the James Hearst Poetry Prize. (Karim 2006: 347)

Layli Arbab Shirani studied law at UC Hastings in San Francisco (Karim 2006: 347). She has translated a selection of the poems of Forugh Farrokhzad which appeared in the online journal *foroug-farrokhzad.org* (*Border Walls*). She was also the co-editor of *Rebels With A Cause: The Failure of the Left in Iran* by Maziar Behrooz (2000) published by I.B. Tauris.

Sheila Shirazi lives in New York City. She was born in Washington, DC. and spent her childhood in Indonesia. (Karim 2006: 347) She has written for *The Iranian* and has worked as assistant editor in the films *Do I Sound Gay?* (2014), *Seeds of Time* (2013), *Inside Job* (2010), *Winter's Bone* (2010) and as writer and associate producer of *Arusi: Persian Wedding* (2009). (*NYTimes*)

Kandi Tayebi is associate vice president for academic affairs, dean of graduate studies, and Professor of English at Sam Houston State University. She finished her B.A. and M.A. at University of Northern Colorado and her PhD at University of Denver (*Shsu.edu*). Her creative writing has appeared in journals such as the *Georgia Review*. (Karim 2006: 347)

Roxanne Varzi left her home town Tehran for the United States after the Islamic Revolution of Iran (*Varzi*). She holds a PhD in anthropology from Columbia University and is currently an Associate professor of anthropology at UC Irvine. Her book *Blurring Souls: Youth, Media and Martyrdom in Post-Revolutionary Iran,* is published by Duke University Press in 2006. (*UC Irvine, Varzi*)

Sholeh Wolpé is a poet, artist, and literary translator. She was born in Iran and lived in Trinidad and the U.K. before moving to the United States. She holds an MA in Radio, Television, and Film from Northwestern University, and a master of Health Sciences degree from Johns Hopkins University. She has several collections of poetry, including *Keeping Time with Blue Hyacinths* (2013), *Rooftops of Tehran* (2008), and *The Scar Saloon* (2004). She translated and edited *Sin: Selected Poems of Forugh Farrokhzad* (2007), which was a recipient of the Lois Roth Persian Translation Award, and her anthology *The Forbidden: Poems from Iran and Its Exiles* won the 2013 Midwest Book Award. She is a regional editor for the Iran section of *Tablet & Pen: Literary Landscapes from the Modern Middle East* (2010). Her co-translation of Walt Whitman's *Song of Myself* in Persian was published on *Whitman Web*. She taught literary translation and poetry at Stonecoast's MFA program. (*The Poetry Foundation*)

Mehri Yalfani was born in Hamadan and moved to Tehran to study electrical engineering at the Technical Faculty of Tehran. After graduation she worked as an engineer for two decades. She immigrated to France in 1985 and to Canada in 1987. She has published several works in Farsi. Her works in English include *Parastoo: Stories and Poems*, published by Women's Press (1995), *Two Sisters: Stories*, published by TSAR (2000), and the novel *Afsaneh's Moon*, published by McGilligan Books (2002). (*Ryerson University*)

Tarssa Yazdani is an author and editor who writes on popular culture, art and music. She is the co-writer of *Hi, How Are You? The Life, Art & Music of Daniel Johnston*, published by Last Gasp of San Francisco (2006). (*Hihowareyou*)

Shahrzad Zahedi was born in Iran. She moved to Switzerland as a child and later to the United States. She holds a PhD in French studies from Brown University and teaches at French Department at

MiraCosta College, USA. She worked as coeditor of the online journal *Equinoxes*. Most of her poems are in French, but recently she also writes in English. (*MiraCosta College*)

Katayoon Zandvakili was born in Tehran. She holds an MFA from Sarah Lawrence College and a BA from UC Berkeley. Her first collection of poetry, *Deer Table Legs*, received the University of Georgia Press Contemporary Poetry Series prize in 1998. Her work has been published in the *Massachusetts Review*, the *Five Fingers Review*, the *Hawaii Review, Rattapallax,* and *Caesura.* It is also anthologized in *A World Between: Poems, Short Stories and Essays by Iranian-Americans* published by George Braziller Inc. (1999) and *American Poetry: The Next Generation* published by Carnegie Mellon (2000). (Karim 2006: 349)

Zarreh was born in Tehran and grew up in London. She holds a BA in sociology and literature from Essex University. She has also a BA in Arabic and Islamic studies from the School of Oriental and African Studies, and a PhD in Islamic mysticism, from the same institute. (Karim 2006: 349)

Shadi Ziaei is a poet and fiction writer. Her poems appeared in *The Iranian*, an online literary journal. She graduated from San Francisco State University's Creative Writing program in 1997. (*The Iranian*)

Afary, J. *Sexual Politics in Modern Iran*. Cambridge University Press, 2009. Print.

Aitchison, C., P. Hopkins, and M.-P. Kwan, eds. *Geographies of Muslim Identities: Diaspora, Gender and Belonging*. Burlington, VT: Ashgate Publishing, 2007.

Amirrezvani, Anita, and Persis M. Karim. *Tremors: New Fiction by Iranian American Writers*. Fayetteville: The University of Arkansas Press, 2013. Print.

Anderson, Benedict R. O. *Imagined Communities: Reflections on the Origin and Spread of Nationalism*. Rev. & ext. ed. London, New York: Verso, 1991. Print.

Anthias, F. &. Yuval-Davis, N. *Racialized Boundaries: Race, Nation, Gender, Colour and Class and the Anti-Racist Struggle*. London/New York: Routledge, 1992. Print.

Appadurai, Arjun. "Disjuncture and Difference in the Global Cultural Economy". *Theory, Culture, Society*. Vol. 7. London: Sage, 1990. 295-310.

Asayesh, Gelareh. *Saffron Sky: A Life between Iran and America*. Boston: Beacon Press, 2002, c1999. Print.

Atkinson, Dwight. *Alternative Approaches to Second Language Acquisition*. 1st ed. London, New York: Routledge, 2011. Print.

Bahrampour, Tara. *To See and See Again: A Life in Iran and America*. 1st ed. New York: Farrar, Straus and Giroux, 1999. Print.

Bakhtin, M. M. *The Dialogic Imagination: Four Essays*. Ed. Michael Holquist. Austin: University of Texas Press, 1981. Print.

Bank Muñoz, C. *Transnational Tortillas: Race, Gender, and Shop-Floor Politics in Mexico and the United States*. Ithaca, NY: Cornell University Press, 2008.

Benstock, S. *The Private Self: Theory and Practice of Women's Auto-

biographical Writings: University of North Carolina Press, 1988. Print.

Bhabha, Homi K. "DissemiNation: Transnationalism." *The Location of Culture*. London: Routledge, 1994. 139-70. Print.

—. *The Location of Culture*. London: Routledge, 1994. Print.

Border Walls, Translated by Layli Arbab Shirani. Web. 12 Dec. 2015. <http://www.forughfarrokhzad.org/selectedworks/ selectedworks3.php>.

Boston Athenæum. Marjan Kamali. Web. 12 Dec. 2015. <http://www.bostonathenaeum.org/library/book-recommendations/ athenaeum-authors/marjan-kamali>.

Bourne, Jenny. "Re: locations-from Bradford to Brighton". *New Formations* 17 (1992): 86-94. Print.

Breen, M., ed. *Learners Contribution to Language Learning: New Directions in Research*. London: Longman/Pearson Education, 2001. Print.

Chodorow, Nancy. *The Reproduction of Mothering: Psychoanalysis and the Sociology of Gender*. Berkeley: University of California Press, 1978. Print.

Cixous, Hélène. *The Hélène Cixous Reader*. Ed. Susan Sellers. New York: Routledge, 1994.

City. Mahru Elahi. Staff, 2011. Web. 11 Dec. 2015. <http://www.es-cat.org/ Staff.html>.

Clifford, James. *Diasporas*, 1994. Print. Cultural Anthropology 9(3).

Constable, N., ed. *Cross-Border Marriages: Gender and Mobility in Trans-national Asia*. Philadelphia: University of Pennsylvania Press, 2005.

Cummins, Jim, and Chris Davison. *International handbook of English language teaching*. New York: Springer, 2007. Print. Springer international handbooks of education 15.

Davies, B., and R. Harré. "Positioning: The Discursive Production of Selves." *Journal for the Theory of Social Behavior* 20(1) (1990): 43-63. Print.

Diba, Farah. *An enduring love: My life with the Shah: a memoir*. New York: Miramax, 2005. Print.

Dumas, Firoozeh. *Funny in Farsi: A memoir of growing up Iranian in America*. New York: Random House Trade Paperbacks, 2004. Print.

Duncan, Nancy. *Bodyspace: Destabilizing Geographies of Gender and Sexuality*. London [u.a.]: Routledge, 1996. Print.

Eakin, P.J. *How Our Lives Become Stories: Making Selves*. Ithaca, NY: Cornell University Press, 1999. Print.

Eckert, Penelope, and Sally McConnell-Ginet. *Language and gender*. Cambridge, New York: Cambridge University Press, 2003. Print.

Ehrlich, S. "Gender as Social Practice: Implications for SLA." *Studies in Second Language Aquisition* 19(4) (1997): 421–46. Print.

Elahi, Babak. "Translating the Self: Language and Identity in Iranian-American Women's Memoirs." *Iranian Studies* 39.4 (2006): 461-80. Print.

—."Fake Farsi: Formulaic Flexibility in Iranian-American Women Writers' Memoirs." MELUS 33:2 (2008): 37-54.

Enayti, Amanda. Enayti, Amanda– Author of "Seeking Serenity". Web. 11 Dec. 2015. <http://amandaenayati.com/>.

Falah, Ghazi-Walid, and Caroline R. Nagel. *Geographies of Muslim Women: Gender, Religion, and Space*. New York, NY ; London: The Guilford Press, 2005. Print.

Farahani, F. *Diasporic narratives of sexuality: identity formation among Iranian-Swedish women*: Coronet Books Inc, 2007. Print.

Firoozehdumas.com. Firoozeh Dumas, author of Laughing Without an Accent and best selling title Funny in Farsi » Bio. Web. 11 Dec. 2015. <http://firoozehdumas.com/about-firoozeh-dumas/>.

Fotouhi, Sanaz. *Literature of the Iranian diaspora: Meaning and identity since the Islamic revolution*. London, New York: I.B. Tauris, 2015, cop. 2015. Print

Freeman, Amy. "Moral Geographies and Women's Freedom: Rethinking Freedom Discourse in the Moroccan Context." *Geographies of Muslim Women: Gender, Religion, and Space*. New York, NY; London: The Guilford Press, 2005. 147-77. Print.

Fuchs, M. *The Text is Myself: Women's Life Writing and Catastrophe*: University of Wisconsin Press, 2004. Print.

Galvin, Brendan. "The Contemporary Poet and the Natural World." *After Confession: Poetry as Autobiography*. Kate Sontag and David Graham. Saint Paul, Minn: Graywolf Press, 2001. Print.

Gardner, Robert C., and Wallace E. Lambert. *Attitudes and motivation in second-language learning*. Rowley, Mass: Newbury House Publishers, 1972. Print.

Ghorashi, Halleh. *Ways to Survive, Battles to Win: Iranian Women Exiles in the Netherlands and United States*. New York: Nova Science Publishers, 2002. Print.

Gilbert, Pamela. "Sex and the Modern City: English Studies and the Spatial Turn." *The Spatial Turn: Interdisciplinary perspectives*. London, New York: Routledge, 2009. 102–21. Print.

Gilmore, Leigh. *The Limits of Autobiography: Trauma and Testimony*. Ithaca N.Y.: Cornell University Press, 2001. Print.

Goodreads Author: Azadeh Moaveni. Web. 12 Dec. 2015. <http://www.goodreads.com/author/show/5134.Azadeh_Moaveni>.

Grassian, Daniel. *Iranian and diasporic literature in the 21st century: A critical study*. Jefferson, N.C.: McFarland & Co, 2013. Print.

Gray, B. *Women and the Irish Diaspora*. New York: Routledge, 2004.

Grewal, I. *Transnational America: Feminisms, Diasporas, Neoliberalisms*. Durham, NC: Duke University Press, 2005.

Griffith, R. M., and B. D. Savage, eds. Women *and Religion in the African Diaspora: Knowledge, Power, and Performance*. Baltimore, MD: Johns Hopkins University Press, 2006.

Grosz, Elizabeth. "Inscriptions and Body Maps: Representations and the Corporeal." *Space, Gender, Knowledge: Feminist Readings*. Ed. Joanne P. Sharp and Linda McDowell. London [etc.]: Arnold, 1997. 236-46. Print.

Hakakian, Roya. *About Roya Hakakian*. Web. 12 Dec. 2015. <http://www.royahakakian.com/about/>.

Hall, Stuart, and K. H Chen. "The Formation of a Diasporic Intellectual: An interview with Stuart Hall." *Stuart Hall: Critical Dialogue in*

Cultural Studies. Ed. D. Morley and K. H. Chen. London and New York: Routledge, 1996. 484-503. Print.

Hanaway, William L. "Half-Voices: Persian Women's Lives and Letters." *Women's Autobiographies in Contemporary Iran.* Afsaneh Najmabadi. Cambridge, Mass.: Harvard University Press, 1990. Print.

Haraway, Donna J. "A Cyborg Manifesto Science, Technology, and Socialist-Feminism in the Late Twentieth Century." *Simians, cyborgs, and women: The reinvention of nature.* New York N.Y.: Routledge, 1991. 149-81. Print.

—. *Simians, cyborgs, and women: The reinvention of nature.* New York (N.Y.): Routledge, 1991. Print.

Harbord, Janet. "Platitudes of Everyday Life?" *Temporalities, Autobiography and Everyday Life.* Eds. J. Campbell & J. Harbord Manchester: Manchester University Press, 2002. 21-34.

Hemami, Taraneh. *About: Taraneh Hemami.* Web.

hihowareyou.com. About the Authors: Tarssa Yazdani. Web. 12 Dec. 2015. <http://www.hihowareyou.com/store/shop/details/464>.

hooks, bell. *Feminist theory from Margin to Center.* Boston, MA: South End Press, 1984. Print.

—. "Choosing the Margin as a Space of Radical Openness." In: *Yearning: Race, Gender, and Cultural Politics.* Toronto, Ont., Canada: Between-the-Lines, 1990. 145-53. Print.

—. *Yearning: Race, Gender, and Cultural Politics.* Toronto, Ont., Canada: Between-the-Lines, 1990. Print.

Hornung, Alfred, and Ernstpeter Ruhe. *Postcolonialism & Autobiography.* Amsterdam: Rodopi, 1998. Print.

Kamkar, Esther. *About Esther Kamkar—Poet, Artist, Writer, Educator, Palo Alto, San Francisco.* Esther Kamkar, 2015. Web. 12 Dec. 2015. <http://www.estherkamkar.com/about.htm>.

Karim, Persis M. *Let Me Tell You Where I've Been: New Writing by Women of the Iranian Diaspora.* Fayetteville, Ark.: University of Arkansas Press, 2006. Print.

Karim, P. M., and M. M. Khorrami. *A World Between: Poems, Short Stories, and Essays by Iranian-Americans.* George Braziller, 1999. Print.

Kenyon Review. Contributors | Haleh Hatami. Web. 12 Dec. 2015. <http://www.kenyonreview.org/journal/winter-2007/contributors/>.

Khaki Gallery. Parinaz Elish: group4. Press Release., 2013. Web. 11 Dec. 2015. <http://www.khakigallery.net/parinazelishgroup4.html>.

Khalvati, Mimi. *Biography.* Khalvati, Mimi, 2014. Web. 12 Dec. 2015. <http://www.mimikhalvati.co.uk/02_biog/biog_1.htm>.

Kraus, W. "The Narrative Negotiation of Identity and Belonging." *Narrative Inquiry* 16(1) (2006): 103-11. Print.

Kristeva, Julia. "Stabat Mater." *The Kristeva Reader.* Ed. Toril Moi. New York: Columbia University Press, 1986. 160-86. Print.

—. *The Kristeva Reader.* Ed. Toril Moi. New York: Columbia University Press, 1986. Print.

—. "Women's Time." *The Kristeva Reader.* Ed. Toril Moi. New York: Columbia University Press, 1986. 187-213. Print.

Labyrinth Books. Let Me Tell You Where I've Been — Contributors. Web. 12 Dec. 2015. <http://www.labyrinthbooks.com/events_detail.aspx?evtid=130>.

Lantolf, J. P. (ed). *Sociocultural Theory and Second Language Learning.* Oxford: Oxford University Press, 2000. Print.

Lionnet, Françoise. *Postcolonial Representations: Women, Literature, Identity.* Ithaca New York: Cornell University Press, 1995. Print.

Lipstick Jihad – eNotes.com. Web. 12 Dec. 2015. <http://www.enotes.com/topics/lipstick-jihad>

Mahdavi, P. *Passionate Uprisings: Iran's Sexual Revolution.* Stanford University Press, 2009. Print.

Malek, Amy. "Memoir as Iranian Exile Cultural Production: A Case Study of Marjane Satrapi's *Persepolis* Series." *Iranian Studies.* Vol. 39, 2006 – Issue 3. 353-380.

Malin, Jo. *The Voice of the Mother: Embedded Maternal Narratives in Twentieth-Century Women's Autobiographies.* Carbondale, Ill.: Southern Illinois University Press, 2000. Print.

Markus, H. N. P. "Possible Selves." *American Psychologist* 41(9) (1986): 954-69. Print.

Massey, Doreen. "Politics and Space/Time." *New Left Review* 196 (1992): 65-84. Print.

—. *Space, Place, and Gender.* Minneapolis: University of Minnesota Press, 1994. Print.

Menard-Warwick, Julia. *Gendered Identities and Immigrant Language Learning.* Bristol, Buffalo: Multilingual Matters, 2009. Print. Critical Language and Literacy Studies 4.

Mernissi, Fatima. *Beyond the Veil: Male-female Dynamics in Modern Muslim Society.* Bloomington: Indiana University Press, 1987.

Metcalf, Barbara D. "Introduction: Sacred Words: Sanctioned Practice, New Communities." *Making Muslim space in North America and Europe.* Ed. Barbara D. Metcalf. Berkeley: University of California Press, 1996. 1–27. Print.

—. *Making Muslim space in North America and Europe.* Ed. Barbara Daly Metcalf. Berkeley: University of California Press, 1996. Print.

Milani, Farzaneh. "Veiled Voices: Women's Autobiographies in Iran." *Women's Autobiographies in Contemporary Iran.* Afsaneh Najmabadi. Cambridge, Mass.: Harvard University Press, 1990. Print.

—. *Veils and words: The Emerging Voices of Iranian Women Writers.* 1st ed. Syracuse, N.Y: Syracuse University Press, 1992. Print.

Miller, Nancy K. *Getting Personal: Feminist Occasions and Other Autobiographical Acts.* New York: Routledge, 1991. Print.

MiraCosta College (MCC). *Zahedi, Shahrzad.* Web.

Moaveni, Azadeh. *Lipstick Jihad: A Memoir of Growing up Iranian in America and American in Iran.* Pbk. ed. New York: PublicAffairs, 2006. Print.

Modarressi, Taghi. "Writing with an Accent." *Chanteh: The Iranian Cross-Cultural Quarterly* 1. 1992: 7-9.

Moghissi, H., and H. Ghorashi. *Muslim Diaspora in the West: Negotiating Gender, Home and Belonging:* Ashgate, 2010. Print.

Moore, Henrietta L. *A Passion for Difference: Essays in Anthropology and Gender*. Cambridge: Polity, 1994. Print.

Montréal, arts interculturels (MAI). *Nika Khanjani*, 2015. Web. 12 Dec. 2015. <http://m-a-i.qc.ca/en/index.php?id=412>.

Morley D. and K. H. Chen (eds). *Stuart Hall: Critical Dialogue in Cultural Studies*. London and New York: Routledge, 1996. Print

Moshiri, Farnoosh. *Author: Farnoosh Moshiri*, 2015. Web. 12 Dec. 2015. <http://www.farnooshmoshiri.net/>.

Motlagh, Amy. "Towards a Theory of Iranian American Life Writing". *MELUS* Vol. 33. No. 2 Iranian American Literature, 2008): 17-36. Print.

Naficy, Hamid. *The Making of Exile Cultures: Iranian Television in Los Angeles*. Minneapolis: University of Minnesota Press, 1993. Print.

Nafisi, Azar. *Reading Lolita in Tehran*. New York: Random House, 2003. Print.

Najmabadi, Afsaneh. *Women's Autobiographies in Contemporary Iran*. Cambridge, Mass.: Harvard University Press, 1990. Print.

Nationalisms and Sexualities. Edited by Andrew Parker, Mary Russo, Doris Sommer, and Patricia Yaeger. New York: Routledge, 1992.

Navab, Aphrodite D. *Aphrodite Désirée Navab: Bio*, 2014. Web. 12 Dec. 2015. <http://aphroditenavab.net/bio.html>.

Normandale AFA. Dowlatshahi, Layla. Faculty Bios | Normandale AFA in Creative Writing on WordPress.com. Web. 11 Dec. 2015. <https://normandaleafacw.wordpress.com/faculty-author-bios/>.

Norton, B. &. A. P. T. P., ed. *Gender and English Language Learners*. Alexandria, VA: TESOL Publications, 2004. Print.

Norton, Bonny. *Identity and Language Learning: Gender, Ethnicity and Educational Change*. Harlow: Pearson Education, 2000. Print. Language in social life series.

—. "Non-Participation, Imagined Community and the Language Classroom." *Learners Contribution to Language Learning: New Directions in Research*. Ed. M. Breen. London: Longman/Pearson Education, 2001. 159–71. Print.

—, and Carolyn McKinney. "An Identity Approach to Second Language

Aquisition." *Alternative Approaches to Second Language Acquisition.* 1st ed. London, New York: Routledge, 2011. 73-94. Print.

—, and A. Pavlenko. "Gender and English Language Learners: Challemges and Possibilities." *Gender and English Language Learners.* Ed. B. &. A. P. T. P. Norton. Alexandria, VA: TESOL Publications, 2004. Print.

NYTimes.com. Sheila Shirazi – Filmography – Movies & TV – Web. 12 Dec. 2015. <http://www.nytimes.com/movies/person/1671663/Sheila-Shirazi/filmography>.

O'Connor, Maureen. *Life Stories: A Guide to Reading Interests in Memoirs, Autobiographies, and Diaries.* Oxford: ABC-CLIO, LLC, 2011. Print.

Pavlenko, A., and J. Lantolf. "Second Language Learning as Participation and the (Re)Construction of Selves." *Sociocultural Theory and Second Language Learning.* Ed. J. P. Lantolf. Oxford: Oxford University Press, 2000. 155-78. Print.

—, and Bonny Norton. "Imagined Communities, Identity and English Language Learning." *International Handbook of English Language Teaching.* New York: Springer, 2007. 669-80. Print. Springer International Handbooks of Education 15.

Peckham, P. H. "Introduction." 711. Web. 11 Dec. 2015. <https://conservancy.umn.edu/bitstream/handle/11299/166081/Atefat-Peckham,%20Susan.pdf?sequence=1&isAllowed=y>.

Perihelion. Farnaz Fatemi, 2014. Web. 11 Dec. 2015. <http://perihelionreview.com/poet_main_s12/fatemi.htm>.

Persiskarim.com. Persis Karim: About. Web. 12 Dec. 2015. <http://persiskarim.com/dev/about/>.

Peyvand. Haale's "Psychedelic Sufi Trance Rock" Music, 2013. Web. 11 Dec. 2015. <http://www.payvand.com/news/09/feb/1011.html>.

Pomona College Magazine. Immigrant Stories: Amy Motlagh. Web. 12 Dec. 2015. <http://magazine.pomona.edu/2012/summer/immigrant-stories/>.

Rapport, Nigel, and Andrew Dawson. *Migrants of Identity: Perceptions of Home in a World of Movement.* Ed. Nigel Rapport and Andrew Dawson. Oxford, UK; New York: Berg, 1998. Print.

—. "The Topic and the Book." *Migrants of Identity: Perceptions of Home in a*

World of Movement. Ed. Nigel Rapport and Andrew Dawson. Oxford, UK; New York: Berg, 1998. 3-19. Print.

Rayaprol, Aparna. *Negotiating Identities: Women in the Indian Diaspora.* Oxford: Oxford University Press, 1997.

Rose, Gillian. "As If the Mirrors Had Blend: Masculine Dwelling, Masculinist Theory and Feminist Masquerade." *Bodyspace: Destabilizing Geographies of Gender and Sexuality.* London [et al.]: Routledge, 1996. 56-86. Print.

Rowbotham, Sheila. *Woman's Consciousness, Man's World.* Harmondsworth: Penguin, 1973. Print. CIC Women's Studies Preservation Project v. 62, no. 3.

Rushdie, Salman. *Imaginary Homelands: Essays and Criticism, 1891–1991.* London, London: Penguin; Granta Books, 1991. Print.

Ryerson University, Asian Heritage. Mehri Yalfani. Web. 12 Dec. 2015. <http://library.ryerson.ca/asianheritage/authors/yalfani/>.

Sahu, Nandini. *The Post-Colonial Space: Writing the Self and the Nation.* New Delhi: Atlantic Publishers, 2007. Print.

Said, E. W. *Reflections on Exile: And Other Literary and Cultural Essays*: Granta Books, 2001. Print.

—. "Reflections on Exile." In: *Reflections on Exile: And Other Literary and Cultural Essays.* Granta Books, 2001. 173-86. Print.

Santa Cruz Life. Tara Fatemi Walker. Web. 11 Dec. 2015. <http://santacruzlife.com/author/tara/>.

Schiffrin, Deborah. "Narrative as Self-Portrait: Sociolinguistic Constructions of Identity." *Language in Society* (1996). Print.

Sedghi, Hamideh. *Women and Politics in Iran.* Cambridge University Press, 2007. Print.

Sharp, Joanne P. "Gendering Nationhood: A Feminist Engagement with National Identity." *Bodyspace: Destabilizing Geographies of Gender and Sexuality.* London [u.a.]: Routledge, 1996. 97-108. Print.

Sharp, Joanne P., and Linda McDowell, eds. *Space, Gender, Knowledge: Feminist Readings.* London [etc.]: Arnold, 1997. Print.

Shsu.edu. Kandi Tayebi's homepage. Web. 12 Dec. 2015.
<http://www.shsu.edu/eng_kat/>.

Silliman, Jael Miriam. *Jewish Portraits, Indian Frames: Women's Narratives from a Diaspora of Hope.* Brandeis University Press; University Press of New England, 2001.

Smashwords. About Mojdeh Marashi. Web. 12 Dec. 2015.
<https://www.smashwords.com/profile/view/Mojdeh>.

Smith, Barbara, ed. *Home Girls: A Black Feminist Anthology.* New York: Kitchen Table: Women of Color Press, 1983. Print.

SOAS, University of London. Professor Laleh Khalili | Staff. Web. 12 Dec. 2015. <http://www.soas.ac.uk/staff/staff36189.php>.

Sontag, Kate, and David Graham. *After Confession: Poetry as Autobiography.* Saint Paul, Minn.: Graywolf Press, 2001. Print.

Soomekh, Saba. *From the Shahs to Los Angeles: Three Generations of Iranian Jewish Women between Religion and Culture.* New York: State University of New York Press, 2013

Spivak, Gayatri Chakravorty. "Can the Subaltern Speak?" *Colonial Discourse and Post-colonial Theory: A Reader.* Ed. Patrick Williams and Laura Chrisman. New York: Columbia University Press, 1994. Print.

Stone, Laurie. *Close to the Bone: Memoirs of Hurt, Rage, and Desire.* 1st ed. New York: Grove Press, 1997. Print.

Stories on Stage Davis. Azin Arefi. Web. 12 Dec. 2015.
<http://storiesonstagedavis.com/?tag=azin-arefi>.

Talbot, Mary M. *Language and Gender.* 2nd ed. Cambridge, UK, Malden, MA: Polity Press, 2010. Print.

Tonkiss, Fran. *Space, the City and Social Theory.* Cambridge: Polity, 2005. Print.

UC Irvine: Rahimieh, Nasrin: Faculty Profile System. Web. 12 Dec. 2015.
<http://www.faculty.uci.edu/profile.cfm?faculty_id=5357>.

The Iranian. Writers, Shadi Ziaei, 2012. Web. 12 Dec. 2015.
<http://iranian.com/ShadiZiaei/>.

—. *iranian.com: Leyla Momeny,* 2014. Web. 12 Dec. 2015.
<http://iranian.com/momeny.html>.

—. *Elham Gheytanchi*, 2014. Web. 11 Dec. 2015. <http://iranian.com/gheytanchi.html>.

The Poetry Foundation. Sholeh Wolpé. Web. 12 Dec. 2015. <http://www.poetryfoundation.org/bio/sholeh-wolpe>.

UC Irvine: Varzi, Roxanne: Faculty Profile System, 2015. Web. 12 Dec. 2015. <http://www.faculty.uci.edu/profile.cfm?faculty_id=5393>.

University of Pennsylvania, Department of History. Firoozeh Kashani-Sabet. Web. 12 Dec. 2015. <http://www.history.upenn.edu/people/faculty/firoozeh-kashani-sabet>.

University of Virginia. Asia Institute, Zjaleh Hajibashi. Web. 12 Dec. 2015. <http://artsandsciences.virginia.edu/asiainstitute/people/southasia/zh2f.html>.

University of Southern California. Faculty Profile: Mitra Parineh: Dana and David Dornsife College of Letters, Arts and Sciences. Web. 12 Dec. 2015. <http://dornsife.usc.edu/cf/faculty-and-staff/faculty.cfm?pid=1016326>.

Varzi, Roxane. *About Roxanne Varzi*, 2015. Web. 12 Dec. 2015. <http://www.socsci.uci.edu/~rvarzi/bio.html>.

Vertovec, Steven. *Transnationalism*. London, New York: Routledge, 2009. Print.

Migration, Diasporas and Transnationalism. Ed. Steven Vertovec and Robin Cohen. Aldershot: Edward Elgar, 1999. Print.

Vickery, Ann. *Leaving Lines of Gender: A Feminist Genealogy of Language Writing*. Hanover, NH: Wesleyan University Press, 2000. Print.

Wagenknecht, Maria D. *Constructing Identity in Iranian-American Self-Narrative*. Palgrave Macmillan, 2015.

Warf, Barney, and Santa Arias. *The Spatial Turn: Interdisciplinary Perspectives*. London, New York: Routledge, 2009. Print.

Warner, R. S. "Immigration and Religious Communities in the United States." *Gatherings in Diaspora: Religious Communities and the New Immigration*. Ed. R. S. Warner and J. G Wittner. Philadelphia: Temple University Press, 1998. 3-34. Print.

Wegner, E. *Communities of Practice: Learning, Meaning and Identity*. Cambridge, MA: Cambridge University Press, 1998. Print.

Werbner, Pnina. "Introduction: The Materiality of Diaspora: Between Aesthetic and 'Real' Politics." *Diaspora* 9, 2000. 1-20.

Williams, Patrick, and Laura Chrisman. *Colonial Discourse and Post-Colonial Theory: A Reader*. New York: Columbia University Press, 1994. Print.

Wilson, Elizabeth. *The Sphinx in the City: Urban Life, the Control of Disorder, and Women*. London: Virago, 1991. Print.

Wong, Y. & Tsai, J. L. (2007). "*Cultural Models of Shame and Guilt*". In J. Tracy, R. Robins & J. Tangney (eds.). *Handbook of Self-Conscious Emotions*, 210-223.

Words Without Borders. Zara Houshmand—Words Without Borders. Web. 12. Dec. 2015. <http://www.wordswithoutborders.org/contributor/zara-houshmand>.

Yang, M. M.-h., ed. *Spaces of their Own: Women's Public Sphere in Transnational China*. Minneapolis: University of Minnesota Press, 1999.

Zielke, B. & J. Straub. "Culture, Psychotherapy/Diasporic Self". *Meaning in Action: Constructions, Narratives, and Representations*. Eds. Toshio Sugiman, Kenneth J. Gergen, Wolfgang Wagner, Yoko Yamada Japan: Springer 2008. Print.

Index

Studien zum Modernen Orient

SMO 13
Fawzi Habashi
Prisoner of All Generations
My Life in the Homeland Egypt
Berlin 2011. Pb. 292 pp., 978-3-87997-350-7

SMO 14
Melanie Krebs
Zwischen Handwerkstradition und globalem Markt
Kunsthandwerker in Uzbekistan und Kirgistan
Berlin 2011. Br. 248 S., 978-3-87997-379-8

SMO 17
Nadine Kreitmeyr
Der Nahostkonflikt durch die Augen Ḥanẓalas
Stereotypische Vorstellungen im Schaffen
des Karikaturisten Naǧi al-ʿAli
Berlin 2012. Br. 140 S., 978-3-87997-402-3

SMO 18
Yuriy Malikov
Tsars, Cossacks, and Nomads
The Formation of a Borderland Culture in Northern Kazakhstan
in the 18th and 19th Centuries
Berlin 2011. Pb. 321 pp., 978-3-87997-359-8

SMO 19
Claus Schönig/Ramazan Çalık/Hatice Bayraktar (Hg.)
Türkisch-deutsche Beziehungen
Perspektiven aus Vergangenheit und Gegenwart
Berlin 2012. Br. 426 S., 978-3-87997-386-6

SMO 20
Ariela Gross
Reaching *wa'y*
Mobilization & Recruitment in Hizb al-Tahrir al-Islami
A Case Study Conducted in Beirut
Berlin 2012. Pb. 111 pp., 978-3-87997-405-4

Studien zum Modernen Orient

SMO 21

Christiane Czygan

Zur Ordnung des Staates

Jungosmanische Intellektuelle und ihre Konzepte
in der Zeitung Hürriyet (1868–1870)
Berlin 2012. Br. 328 S., 978-3-87997-407-8

SMO 23

Tobias Lang

Die Drusen in Libanon und Israel

Geschichte, Konflikte und Loyalitäten
einer religiösen Gemeinschaft in zwei Staaten
Berlin 2013. Br. 174 S., 978-3-87997-416-0

SMO 24

Mary Beth Wilson

Impacts of Participatory Development in Afghanistan

A Call to Reframe Expectations
Berlin 2013. Pb. 526 pp., 978-3-87997-431-3

SMO 27

Amer Nizar Ghrawi

An Elusive Hope

State Reform in Syria, 2000–2007
Berlin 2015. Pb. 381 pp., 978-3-87997-444-3

SMO 29

Britt Ziolkowski

Die Aktivistinnen der Ḥamās

Zur Rolle der Frauen in einer islamistischen Bewegung
Berlin 2017. Pb. 479 pp., 978-3-87997-458-0

Klaus Schwarz Verlag GmbH • Fidicinstr. 29 • D-10965 Berlin
Tel. +30-916 82 749 +30-916 82 751 • Fax +30-322 51 83
www.klaus-schwarz-verlag.com
info@klaus-schwarz-verlag.com